PREMIUM
NOVELTIES

Premium Novelties

©2009 PIE BOOKS

PIE BOOKS

2-32-4, Minami-Otsuka, Toshima-ku, Tokyo 170-0005 Japan
Phone: +81-3-5395-4811   Fax: +81-3-5395-4812
e-mail: editor@piebooks.com
sales@piebooks.com
http://www.piebooks.com

ISBN978-4-89444-752-3 C3070
Printed in Japan

はじめに
Foreward

「ノベルティ」とは、広告や宣伝のために無料配布するボールペン、カレンダー、メモなどのグッズのことを指します。その最も重要な役割は、より多くの人に宣伝対象のことを知ってもらうこと、興味をもってもらうことです。

しかし、一概にノベルティといっても、既製品への簡単な名入れのものから、オリジナルデザインのものまで、その形状はさまざま。街中に販促物が溢れる昨今、人々の心に訴えかけ、「欲しい」と思うノベルティを作り出すことは、容易ではありません。

本書では、街頭・店頭で無料配布されたものから、新商品のプロモーション、商品購入時や懸賞応募時にもらえるグッズまで、さまざまな目的のために制作された、魅力的なノベルティを特集します。これらの作品から、ワクワクする気持ちを呼び起こす、ノベルティ制作のヒントを感じ取っていただけたなら幸いです。

またこの場を借りて、お忙しい中、長期にわたり快くご協力いただきました出品者の皆様に、心より御礼申し上げます。

ピエ・ブックス 編集部

Novelty goods are free items such as ballpoint pens, calendars and note pads that are distributed as a way of advertising or promoting something. Their most important role is to inform as many people as possible about what is being advertised and to capture the interest of those people.

However, the general term "novelty" refers to a range of things from items where a company name has simply been inserted onto an already existing product to items that have been originally design. Existing as we do in a world that abounds with a seemingly infinite number of marketing tools, it is no easy task to create a novelty that appeals to the mind and becomes an object of desire.

This book features a selection of beautiful novelty goods produced for various purposes, some for distribution on the street or in stores, others for promoting new products or given to customers who purchase certain products or as prizes in competitions. We hope that they prove to be a source of ideas for the production of your own exciting novelty goods.

We also take this opportunity to express our sincere appreciation the contributors who gave of their precious time so generously.

Editorial Department, Pie Books

EDITORIAL NOTE

A　FRANCK MULLER「BRACK MAGIC」
ノベルティトランプ
FRANCK MULLER : "BRACK MAGIC" novelty cards

B　時計ブランド　Watch brand

C　FRANCK MULLERの新商品「BRACK MAGIC」のプロモーションとして制作されたマジックトランプ。パープルと黄色のパール印刷が施された箱の中に、トランプが納められている。ハート・ダイヤ・スペード・クローバーと数字がそれぞれのトランプにグラフィカルに描かれており、上品なデザインに仕上がっている。

The magic playing cards were produced to promote FRANK MULLER's new product range, "BRACK MAGIC". The cards are inside a purple and yellow pearl print box. Graphics have been used to draw the hearts, diamonds, spades, clubs and numerals on each card to produce an elegant design.

D　配布対象：イベント会場来場者　配布方法・場所：新商品イベント会場
制作数：3,000個　狙い・効果：新商品の告知とブランドイメージの伝達
Target market : Event guests
Distribution method and area : Event venues　**Number produced** : 3,000
Aim and effect : Communication of the brand's image and concept for the promotion of new products

E　CL：ワールド通商　World Commerce Corporation
AD：美澤 修　Osamu Misawa　D：梶谷聡美　Satomi Kajitani
SB：omdr Co., Ltd.　Japan

F

A　作品タイトル名　Title of work

B　クライアント業種名　Client's type of industry

C　デザインコンセプト　Design concept

D　配布対象 / 配布方法・場所 / 制作数 / 狙い・効果 / 制作コスト
Target market / Distribution method and area /
Number produced / Aim and effect / Production costs

上記以外の制作者呼称は省略せずに掲載しています。
All other production titles are unabbreviated.

E　スタッフクレジット　Creative Stuff

CL：クライアント　Client
CD：クリエイティブ・ディレクター　Creative Director
AD：アート・ディレクター　Art Director
D：デザイナー　Designer
P：フォトグラファー　Photographer
I：イラストレーター　Illustrator
CW：コピーライター　Copywriter
DF：制作会社　Design Firm
SB：作品提供社　Submittor

F　制作国　Country from which submitted

CONTENTS

Q-pot. 展示会プレスキット 「A Christmas Cake!」

Q-pot. : Press kit "A Christmas Cake!"

アクセサリー Accessory

クリスマスケーキをイメージし、Q-pot.のユニークな世界観で作られた五感で楽しむアートブック。仕掛けが随所に散りばめられており、親子でも楽しめる作りになっている。飛び出す仕掛けいっぱいの絵本にはネックレスや物語をイメージしたオリジナルCDもセットになっているスペシャルな作品。本のカバーは金箔・エンボス加工で、かわいい中にも「高級感」や「特別感」を感じさせる。収納するケースにはまるで本物のスイーツのような箱型缶ケースを採用。

An art book for the five senses to relish in the image of a Christmas cake and created with the unique Q-pot perspective. Part of a special production, the picture book with surprise gimmicks throughout that make the book fun for parents and children alike also comes with an original CD based on an image of necklaces and fairytales. The cover of the book contains gold leaf and embossing and is cute as well as exuding a sense of quality and being something out-of-the-ordinary. The metal box in which it is packaged looks for all the world like a real confectionary box.

CL, SB：キューポット Q-pot.　Q-pot. Designer：ワカマツタダアキ
Tadaaki Wakamatsu　CD, AD, D, I：カワムラヒデオ　Hideo Kawamura
P：柴田文子　Fumiko Shibata　Stylist：相澤 樹　Miki Aizawa
Hair Make：橘 房図　Fusae Tachibana　Japan

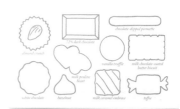

Q-pot. × Harbour City
チャリティーイベントノベルティ

Q-pot. × Harbour City：Charity event novelty

アクセサリー　Accessory

香港の巨大ショッピングモール「Harbour City（ハーバーシティ）」で行われたチャリティーイベントで、世界のデザイナーの中から、2006年度はQ-pot.デザイナー・ワカマツタダアキが選ばれ、チャリティー企画限定のオリジナルポーチをデザイン。イベント期間中、ハーバーシティでHK$1,500以上購入した人を対象に、このポーチをプレゼントした。売上の一部が「Hong Kong Blood Cancer Foundation（香港白血病基金）」へ寄付された。

In 2006 Q-pot designer, Tadaaki Wakamatsu selected from a group of international designers, designed an original pouch exclusively for the charity event held in the huge Harbour City shopping mall in Hong Kong. During the event period, the pouch was presented to people who spent HK$1,500 or more at Harbour City. A portion of the takings was donated to the Hong Kong Blood Cancer Foundation.

配布対象：累計でHK$1,500以上の商品購入者
配布方法・場所：ハーバーシティ
Target market：Customers who spent HK$1,500 or more
Distribution method and area：Harbour City

CL, SB：キューポット　Q-pot.
Q-pot. Designer：ワカマツタダアキ　Tadaaki Wakamatsu
Japan

Q-pot. 店頭プレゼントキャンペーン　Q-pot. : Store gift campaign

アクセサリー　Accessory

Q-pot.の各店舗で商品購入者を対象に行われたプレゼントキャンペーン。フランスパン型のボールペンは、パンをモチーフとした「パンパカパンシリーズ」発売イベントの際に制作した。その他にも、上から見ると梅の花のデザインになっているカップ＆ソーサーやアンティーク調の「Q」のロゴがデザインされているハート型キャンドルなど、ブランドの世界観が感じられるグッズとなっている。

A gift campaign for customers of Q-pot products at its various stores. The baguette-shaped ballpoint pen was produced for the bread-motifed "PANPAKAPAN" series released. Other goods that demonstrate the unique Q-pot. perspective include a cup and saucer set that has a plum blossom pattern when viewed from above and a heart-shaped candle designed with an antique-style logo.

配布対象： [a] 伊勢丹新宿店 パンパカパンシリーズ発売イベント ¥10,000以上の購入者・[b] 阪急うめだ本店オープン記念 ¥20,000以上の購入者・[c] 伊勢丹新宿店 クリスマスイベント ¥20,000以上の購入者
狙い・効果： 新作の訴求や顧客の呼び込み・世界観の打ち出し
Target market : [a] Customers who spend ¥10,000 or more at the Isetan Shinjuku PANPAKAPAN series release event　[b] Customers who spend ¥20,000 at the event commemorating the opening of the Umeda Hankyu store　[c] Customers who spend ¥20,000 or more at the Isetan Shinjuku Christmas event　**Aim and effect :** Marketing a new product and attracting customers, articulation of the brand's world view

CL, SB：キューポット　Q-pot.　Q-pot. Designer：ワカマツタダアキ　Tadaaki Wakamatsu　Japan

a

b

c

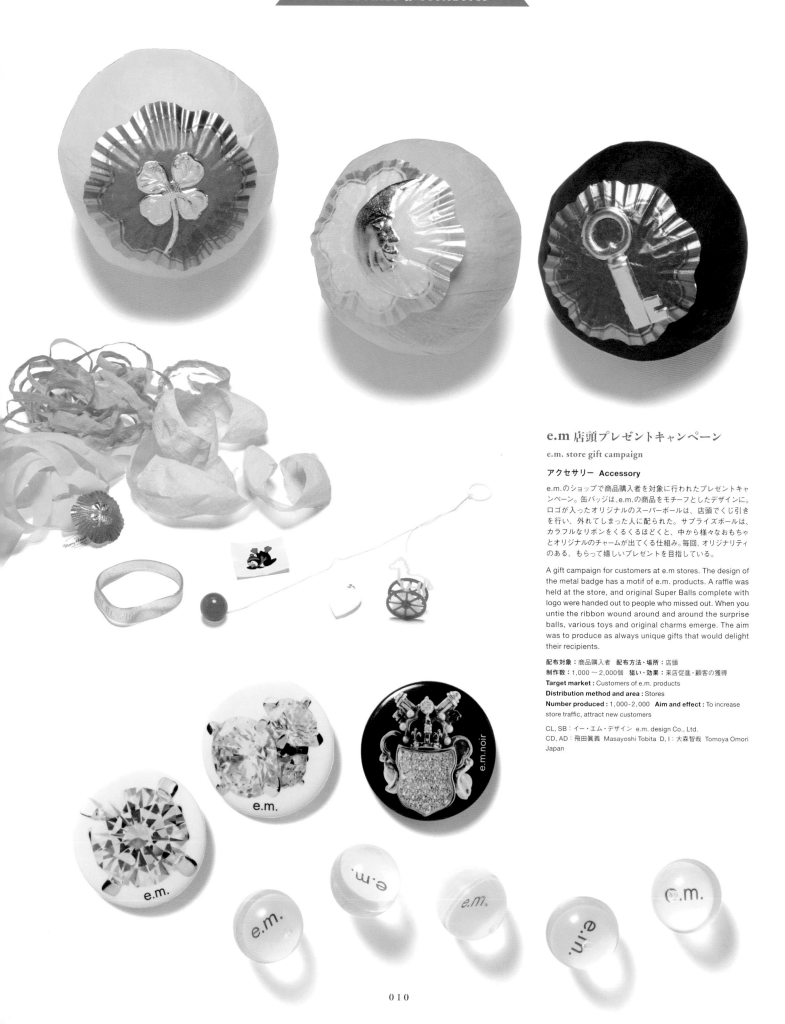

e.m 店頭プレゼントキャンペーン

e.m. store gift campaign

アクセサリー　Accessory

e.m.のショップで商品購入者を対象に行われたプレゼントキャンペーン。缶バッジは、e.m.の商品をモチーフとしたデザインに。ロゴが入ったオリジナルのスーパーボールは、店頭でくじ引きを行い、外れてしまった人に配られた。サプライズボールは、カラフルなリボンをくるくるほどくと、中から様々なおもちゃとオリジナルのチャームが出てくる仕組み。毎回、オリジナリティのある、もらって嬉しいプレゼントを目指している。

A gift campaign for customers at e.m stores. The design of the metal badge has a motif of e.m. products. A raffle was held at the store, and original Super Balls complete with logo were handed out to people who missed out. When you untie the ribbon wound around and around the surprise balls, various toys and original charms emerge. The aim was to produce as always unique gifts that would delight their recipients.

配布対象：商品購入者　配布方法・場所：店頭
制作数：1,000 ～ 2,000個　狙い・効果：来店促進・顧客の獲得
Target market : Customers of e.m. products
Distribution method and area : Stores
Number produced : 1,000-2,000　**Aim and effect :** To increase store traffic, attract new customers

CL, SB：イー・エム・デザイン e.m. design Co., Ltd.
CD, AD：飛田眞義 Masayoshi Tobita　D, I：大森智哉 Tomoya Omori
Japan

e.m.「tiptoe」クリスマスDM
e.m. "tiptoe" Christmas DM

アクセサリー Accessory

子どもから大人まで身につけることのできるアクセサリーをコンセプトとしたブランド、「tiptoe」。毎年、顧客に向けてクリスマスのプレゼント付き挨拶状を贈っている。2007年は、スカルをモチーフとしたプラスチックのキーホルダーをシュリンクし、そのまま郵送。ひと目で「tiptoe」からのDMだと分かる、もらって嬉しい挨拶状となっている。

The brand "tiptoe," whose concept is an accessory that can be used by children and adults alike. A greeting card with a Christmas present attached is given to customers every year. In 2007, a plastic key ring with a scull motif was shrink-wrapped and sent to customers. Customers are certainly delighted to receive the season's greetings card when they realize it is direct mail from tiptoe.

配布対象：顧客　配布方法・場所：郵送　制作数：3,000個　狙い・効果：来店促進
Target market : Customers　**Distribution method and area :** Mail
Number produced : 3,000　**Aim and effect :** To increase store traffic

CL, SB：イー・エム・デザイン e.m. design Co., Ltd.
CD, AD：飛田眞義 Masayoshi Tobita　D, I：大森智哉 Tomoya Omori　Japan

モッズヘア「エマルジョン・ワックス」プレスキット
Mod's Hair : "Emulsion Wax" press kit

消費財メーカー Consumer goods maker

新商品発売に伴い製作されたビニールバッグ。エマルジョン・ワックスのイメージカラーである緑・黄色・オレンジを使ったデザインで、もらった後も普段使いできるように配慮している。

The plastic bag produced in conjunction with a new product release. The bag's design uses the emulsion wax's image colors of green, yellow and orange, the intention being that the bag be put to everyday use after it has served its purpose as part of the press kit.

配布対象：プレス関係者　配布方法・場所：郵送　狙い・効果：プレスキットとしてもらった後も、使いたくなるバッグを目指した
Target market : Media-related people　**Distribution method and area :** Mail
Aim and effect : The aim was that people would want to continue to use the bag after it has served its purpose as part of the press kit.

CL：ユニリーバ・ジャパン Unilever Japan K.K　AD, D：澤田千尋 Chihiro Sawada
Agency：サニーサイドアップ SUNNY SIDE UP Inc.
DF, SB：アンテナグラフィックベース ANTENNA GRAPHIC BASE Co., Ltd.　Japan

ポール＆ジョー
「2008 Christmas Creation」
プレゼントキャンペーン

Paul & Joe "2008 Christmas Creation" gift campaign

化粧品 Cosmetics

2008年冬限定のフェイスカラー＆リップスティックキットと同時期にスタートしたGWPリングノート。リングノートは、オリジナルポーチ同様、レトロなキャットプリントが施されている。

A spiral-bound notebook presented to customers of the face color & lipstick kit, a limited product for winter 2008. The notebook has the same girly cat design as the original pouch.

配布対象：商品購入者　配布方法・場所：店頭
狙い・効果：新規購買者の獲得・購買促進
Target market : Purchasers　**Distribution method and area** : Stores
Aim and effect : Sales promotion

CL, SB：アルビオン　ポール＆ジョー ボーテ
　　　　ALBION co., ltd.　PAUL & JOE BEAUTE　Japan

ポール＆ジョー
「VACANCES COLLECTION 2008」
プレゼントキャンペーン

Paul & Joe "Vacances Collection 2008" gift campaign

化粧品 Cosmetics

ポール＆ジョーの2008年のテーマは、「FLIRT」。期間中に税込￥8,400以上の商品を購入した人を対象に、淡いピンクと茶色の色合いがノスタルジックな、オリジナルトラベルポーチがプレゼントされた。

Paul & Joe's theme for 2008 is "FLIRT." Customers who purchase products to the value of ¥8,400 more (tax included) throughout the campaign period received an original nostalgic travel pouch in light pink and brown.

配布対象：商品購入者　配布方法・場所：店頭
狙い・効果：新規購買者の獲得・来店促進
Target market : Purchasers
Distribution method and area : Stores　**Aim and effect** : Sales promotion

CL, SB：アルビオン　ポール＆ジョー ボーテ
　　　　ALBION co., ltd.　PAUL & JOE BEAUTE　Japan

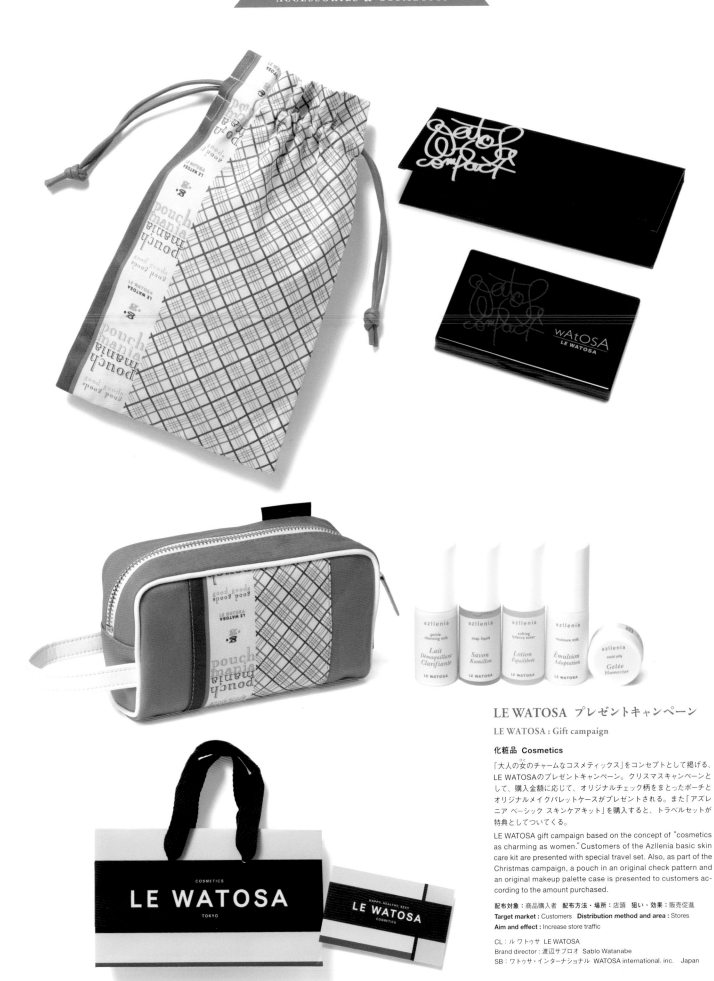

LE WATOSA プレゼントキャンペーン

LE WATOSA : Gift campaign

化粧品 Cosmetics

「大人の女のチャームなコスメティックス」をコンセプトとして掲げる、LE WATOSAのプレゼントキャンペーン。クリスマスキャンペーンとして、購入金額に応じて、オリジナルチェック柄をまとったポーチとオリジナルメイクパレットケースがプレゼントされる。また「アズレニア ベーシック スキンケアキット」を購入すると、トラベルセットが特典としてついてくる。

LE WATOSA gift campaign based on the concept of "cosmetics as charming as women." Customers of the Azllenia basic skin care kit are presented with special travel set. Also, as part of the Christmas campaign, a pouch in an original check pattern and an original makeup palette case is presented to customers according to the amount purchased.

配布対象：商品購入者　配布方法・場所：店頭　狙い・効果：販売促進
Target market : Customers　Distribution method and area : Stores
Aim and effect : Increase store traffic

CL：ル ワトゥサ LE WATOSA
Brand director：渡辺サブロオ　Sablo Watanabe
SB：ワトゥサ・インターナショナル　WATOSA international. inc.　Japan

資生堂「マジョリカ マジョルカ」2008 プレスキット

Shiseido "Majolica Majorca" : 2008 press kit

化粧品 Cosmetics

「A girl with wings」をテーマに、羽をモチーフとしたプレスキットを作成。ブランドのもつ小悪魔的なイメージや幻想的な世界観がプレスキットだけで伝わるようにデザインされている。箱いっぱいに詰められた鳥の羽は全て紙で表現され、羽の下にはブローチが隠されている。観音開きの箱の下段は引き出せるようになっており、メイクボックスや小物入れとしても活用できる。

The press kit's motif of bird feathers corresponds to the make-up range's theme of "A girl with wings." The brand's devilish image and fanciful view of the world was designed in a way that could be conveyed with just a press kit. The bird feathers that fill the whole box are all made from paper, and underneath them a brooch is concealed. The box has double doors and when the bottom drawer is pulled out, can be used as a makeup box or an accessory case.

配布対象：ファッション雑誌編集者・関係者　**配布方法・場所**：手渡し　**制作数**：200個　**狙い・効果**：ブランドイメージと新製品プロモーションの世界観の伝達

Target market : Fashion magazine editors and related persons　**Distribution method and area** : Hand delivery
Number produced : 200　**Aim and effect** : Communication of the brand's image and concept for the promotion of new products

CL, SB：資生堂　Shiseido Co., Ltd.　CD, CW：吉田聖子　Shoko Yoshida　AD, D, I：大谷有紀　Yuki Otani
AD：川原彩子　Ayako Kawahara　CW：石川北斗　Hokuto Ishikawa　Japan

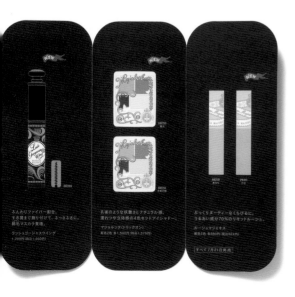

資生堂「マジョリカ マジョルカ」2007 プレスキット
Shiseido "Majolica Majorca": 2007 press kit

化粧品 Cosmetics

「Like a Doll」をテーマに、ドールハウスをモチーフとしたプレスキットを作成。扉を開けると、少女時代を思い起こす、金髪のかわいい人形が現れ、引き出しの中には新商品が納められている。ドールハウスの中に描かれたソファなどの家具もかわいらしく、ブランドイメージを強く印象づけるプレスキットに仕上げられている。

The theme being "Like a Doll," a press kit with a motif of a doll's house was produced. The pretty doll with blonde hair that brings back memories of childhood appears when you open the door, and new products have been placed in the drawers. The furniture including the sofa drawn in the doll's house is also cute. The result is a press kit that leaves a strong impression of the brand's image.

配布対象：ファッション雑誌編集者・関係者　配布方法・場所：手渡し　制作数：200個
狙い・効果：ブランドイメージと新製品プロモーションの世界観の伝達
Target market : Fashion magazine editors and related persons　**Distribution method and area :** Hand delivery　**Number produced :** 200　**Aim and effect :** Communication of the brand's image and concept for the promotion of new products

CL, SB：資生堂 Shiseido Co., Ltd. CD：山本浩司 Koji Yamamoto
AD, D：川原彩子 Ayako Kawahara P：金澤正人 Masato Kanazawa
I：山口 崇 Takashi Yamaguchi CW：吉田聖子 Shoko Yoshida
Japan

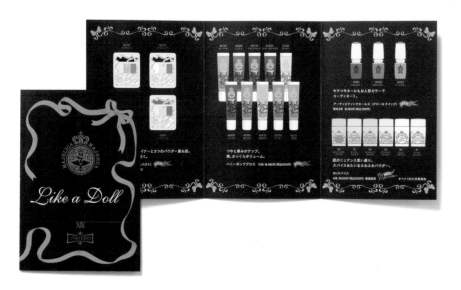

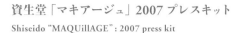

資生堂「マキアージュ」2007 プレスキット
Shiseido "MAQUillAGE" : 2007 press kit

化粧品 Cosmetics

2007年秋のプロモーションテーマ「ハンサムビューティー」をもとに
製作されたCMで、出演モデルがスカーフを格好良く外すシーンがある。
マットな黒い箱を開けると、中には新商品とスカーフのモチーフが折
り込まれており、高級感のあるプレスキットとして仕上げられている。

The commercial produced around the theme of the autumn
promotion 2007 "Handsome Beauty" contains a scene where a
model stylishly removes her scarf. Tucked inside a matte black
box are the new Shiseido products and a motif of a scarf that
impart a sense of high quality to the press kit.

配布対象：ファッション雑誌編集者・関係者　配布方法・場所：手渡し
制作数：400個　狙い・効果：ブランドイメージと新製品プロモーションの世界
観の伝達
Target market : Fashion magazine editors and related persons
Distribution method and area : Hand delivery　**Number produced :** 400
Aim and effect : Communication of the brand's image and concept for
the promotion of new products

CL, SB：資生堂 Shiseido Co., Ltd.　CD, CW：竹内祥記 Yoshiki Takeuchi
D：志賀玲子 Reiko Shiga　CW：吉田聖子 Shoko Yoshida
Printing, Processing：日本写真印刷 Nissha Printing Co., Ltd.　Japan

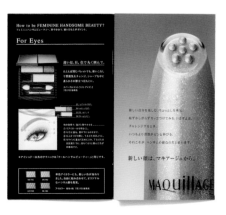

プラチナ・ギルド・インターナショナル
ブランドブック「Words of Platinum」

Platinum Guild International Brand Book
"Words of Platinum"

プラチナ・ジュエリーの広報機関
Platinum jewelry public relations agency

プラチナ・ジュエリーの普及を目指した国際的な広報機関が、2007年にイベントを開催。プラチナの魅力を知ってもらうため、高級感溢れる真っ白なブランドブックが来場者に渡された。中には、ジュエリーボックスをイメージさせる小さな正方形が並んでおり、その一つひとつが「PURE」「ETERNAL」などプラチナの魅力や性質を表す英単語が刻印されたアクリルパネルとブックレットになっている。ブックレットの表紙はすべてを白で統一し、キーワードから連想するビジュアルはエンボス加工とホワイト箔で描かれた。プラチナが持つ純粋さ、品質感を伝えるデザインに仕上がっている。

An international public relations agency aimed at popularizing platinum jewelry that held an event in 2007. To convey the allure of platinum, a pure-white brand book infused with a sense of high quality was handed out to customers. Inside are rows of small squares creating an image of a jewelry box. Each of the squares is an acrylic panel engraved with the English words "pure" and "eternal" and booklets that express the allure and the properties of platinum. The covers of the booklets are all standardized with white and visuals that make an association with keywords have been embossed and drawn on with white foil. The design is finished to convey the purity and quality unique to platinum.

配布対象：イベント来場者　配布方法・場所：会場　制作数：100
狙い・効果：プラチナ・ジュエリーの普及
Target market : Event guests　**Distribution method and area** : Event venues
Number produced : 100　**Aim and effect** : Popularizing platinum jewelry

CL：プラチナ・ギルド・インターナショナル　Platinum Guild International
CD：原田 朋　Tomoki Harada　AD：関谷奈々　Nana Sekiya
D：鈴木 学　Manabu Suzuki / 島田玲奈　Reina Shimada
CW：佐藤恵子　Keiko Sato　Planning, Agency, SB：博報堂　Hakuhodo Inc.
Planning, Agency：アドソルト　ADSALT　Japan

MAMEW オープニングパーティ招待状
MAMEW：Invitation for the launch party

化粧品 Cosmetics

代官山に店舗を構える化粧品ブランド「MAMEW」が関係者に送付した、ショップのオープニングパーティの案内状。化粧貼りの箱を開けると、カメラマン・日下雅貴氏が撮影した「空」のポジフィルム、コピーライター・渡辺潤平氏の文章と日下氏の写真によって構成されたパンフレット、青い鳥の羽、代官山のマップなど、様々なツールが同梱されている。

An invitation sent out to relevant people for the launch party of a store set up by the cosmetics brand MAMEW in Daikanyama. Open the veneer box to find inside various tools including the reversal film for "Sky" shot by photographer Masaki Kusaka; work by copywriter Junpei Watanabe; a pamphlet compiled with photographs by Masaki Kusaka; the feather of a blue bird; and a map of Daikanyama.

配布対象：関係者　配布方法・場所：郵送
Target market : Related persons　**Distribution method and area :** Mail

CL：MAMEW　CD, AD：水野 学 Manabu Mizuno　PR：小野由紀子 Yukiko Ono
D：久能真理 Mari Kuno　P：日下雅貴 Masaki Kusaka
I：土谷尚武 Shobu Tsuchiya　CW：渡辺 潤平 Junpei Watanabe
DF, SB：グッドデザインカンパニー good design company　Japan

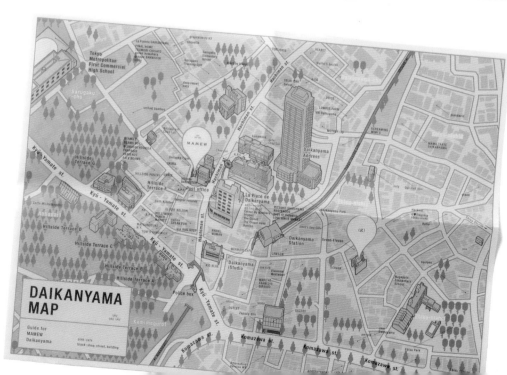

FRANCK MULLER「BRACK MAGIC」
ノベルティトランプ
FRANCK MULLER : "BRACK MAGIC" novelty cards

時計ブランド Watch brand

FRANCK MULLERの新商品「BRACK MAGIC」のプロモーションとして制作されたマジックトランプ。パープルと黄色のパール印刷が施された箱の中に、トランプが納められている。ハート・ダイヤ・スペード・クローバーと数字がそれぞれのトランプにグラフィカルに描かれており、上品なデザインに仕上がっている。

The magic playing cards were produced to promote FRANK MULLER's new product range, "BRACK MAGIC". The cards are inside a purple and yellow pearl print box. Graphics have been used to draw the hearts, diamonds, spades, clubs and numerals on each card to produce an elegant design.

配布対象：イベント会場来場者 **配布方法・場所**：新商品イベント会場
制作数：3,000個 **狙い・効果**：新商品の告知とブランドイメージの伝達
Target market : Event guests
Distribution method and area : Event venues **Number produced** : 3,000
Aim and effect : Communication of the brand's image and concept for the promotion of new products

CL：ワールド通商 World Commerce Corporation
AD：美澤 修 Osamu Misawa D：梶谷聡美 Satomi Kajitani
SB：omdr Co., Ltd. Japan

AHKAH couture maison
プレス発表招待状・プレスキット

Ahkah couture maison :
Media release invitation and press kit

ジュエリー Jewelry

AHKAHの源泉は、「儚く無垢な美しさを追い求め、描き続ける
ジュエリー」。couture maisonは、そんなAHKAHブランドの
オーダーメイドサロンであり、専任のジュエリー・コンシェルジュ
がアドバイスしながら、顧客の希望に沿ったデザインを完成さ
せていく。プレス発表の際には、ブランドブックとともに、繊細
なデザインのネックレスを同封。白と青を基調とした、高級
感溢れるデザインとなっている。

AHKAH's philosophy is "Jewelry that seeks to express an
innocent and fleeting beauty." Couture maison is a made-
to-order salon for the AHKAH brand, staffed with profes-
sional jewelry consultants who provide jewelry advice and
come up with designs in line with customers' ideas. At the
media release, a brand book and a delicately designed
necklace were enclosed in the press kit. The design that
exudes a sense of high quality is based on the color of
white and blue.

配布対象：編集者・顧客　配布方法・場所：パーティ会場
制作数：2,000個　狙い・効果：ブランドイメージの流布
Target market：Editors, customers
Distribution method and area：Party venue
Number produced：2,000　**Aim and effect**：Dissemination of the
brand image

CL：アー・カー AHKAH　D, SB：ストア・インク　Store inc.
P：土井浩一郎　Koichiro Doi
Printing, Processing：池田印刷　Ikeda Printing Co., Ltd.　Japan

JIN's GLOBAL STANDARD
オープニングノベルティ

JIN's GLOBAL STANDARD : Opening novelty

眼鏡ショップ Eyewear retailer

オリジナルメガネ、サングラスを販売するJIN's GLOBAL STANDARD の原宿明治通り店オープニング用のノベルティグッズ。メガネを着用した男女40名のモデルを撮影して一冊にまとめた上製の大型フォトブックが制作された。

Novelty goods for the launch of JIN's GLOBAL STANDARD Harajuku Meiji-dori store which sells original eyewear. A large-size deluxe edition photo book featuring photographs of 40 men and women wearing glasses was produced.

配布対象：関係者・プレス 配布方法・場所：オープニング来場者に限定配布
狙い・効果：大反響を呼び、雑誌各社からの取材件数が倍増した。高品質の眼鏡を低価格で提供していながら、ファッション面でも優れている洗練されたブランドというイメージをアピールすることに成功した

Target market : Related persons, media
Distribution method and area : Limited distribution to guests at the opening **Aim and effect :** It created a sensation and the number of magazines covering the event doubled. A successful appeal with the image of a brand offering high-quality, low-cost eyewear, and in terms of fashion, one that is seriously sophisticated

CL：JIN'S AD：水野 学 Manabu Mizuno D, DF, SB：good design company
P：鈴木 心 Shin Suzuki PR：小野由紀子 Yukiko Ono Japan

LOVE
DREAM PEACE
PRIDE HUMOR TRUTH
HOPE   CHALLENGE   JUSTICE

GLORY   HEART   ONLY   TOMORROW   EVOLUTION

PASSION   IMPRESSION   FUTURE   VICTORY   FRIENDSHIP

FAME   ORDINARY   UNITY   STANDARD   HONOR   TOGETHER   TRUST

PROGRESS   FREEDOM   DUTY   TIME   MERCY   SOUL   CONFIDENCE

BALANCE   FORCE   ADVANCE   EXPERIENCE   POTENTIAL   SPIRIT   SENSE   POSSIBILITY

NATURE   UNIVERSE   HAPPINESS   GLOBAL   FAITH   EARTH   DESTINY   BELIEVE

WONDERFUL   VALUE   CONCEPT   CREATION   IDENTITY   WISH   PERFECT   TRIUMPH   IMAGINATION

SOLUTION   DECISION   CONQUEST   ABSOLUTE   MESSAGE   BELIEF   THINK   ACTIVE   SYMPATHY   PRAY

DESIGN   FOLLOW   UNDERSTAND   SEARCH   LEARN   STUDY   TEACH   NEW   FEEL   CARE   JIN's   DELIGHT   EXCITE   PROMISE

0.1 0.2 0.3 0.4 0.5 0.6 0.7 0.8 0.9 1.0 1.2 1.5 2.0

JINs GLOBAL STANDARD "EYEWEAR IS JIN's"

JIN's GLOBAL STANDARD オープニング インビテーション

JIN's GLOBAL STANDARD : Opening party invitation

眼鏡ショップ Eyewear retailer

オリジナルメガネ、サングラスを販売するJIN's GLOBAL STANDARDの原宿明治通り店オープニング インビテーション。視力検査表を模したポスターと遮眼子がセットになっており、パッケージに貼られたステッカーに、ショップオープンの日付が記載されている。

Invitation to the launch of Jin's Global Standard Harajuku Meiji-dori store selling original eyewear. The date of the launch was inscribed on the sticker attached to the packaging containing an eye chart in the form of a poster and an eye occluder.

配布対象：関係者・プレス 配布方法・場所：郵送 制作数：1,500部 狙い・効果：「インビテーションがかわいかったので目を惹かれて来た」というプレスも多く、来場者数が当初の予想の3倍以上となり、大盛況となった

Target market : Related persons, media **Distribution method and area :** Mail **Number produced :** 1,500
Aim and effect : Many media reps attended because they thought "the invitation was lovely and had caught their attention" and three times as many guests turned up than originally anticipated.

CL：JIN'S AD：水野 学 Manabu Mizuno D, DF, SB：good design company PR：小野由紀子 Yukiko Ono Japan

ヴィダルサスーン
「Fashion × Music × Vidal Sassoon」
プレゼントキャンペーン

"Fashion × Music × Vidal Sassoon" : Gift campaign

消費財メーカー　Consumer goods

ヘアだけでなく、ファッションや音楽業界も巻き込んだヴィダルサスーンの複合型キャンペーン。新商品の発売を機に、ブランドのルーツに立ち戻り、ヴィダルサスーンの歴史を60年代、70年代、80年代の3つで表現している。本キャンペーンでは、安室奈美恵、カリスマスタイリストのパトリシア・フィールド、ヘアスタイリストのオーランド・ピタを起用。各年代のCMや広告で展開している衣装やスタイリングを再現したバービーも製作し、若い世代を取り込むことに成功した。

A multi-facet Vidal Sassoon campaign that involves not only hair but also fashion and music. On the occasion of a new product release, the brand is returning to its roots and recalling the Vidal Sassoon of the 60s, 70s and 80s. The campaign features Namie Amuro; charisma stylist, Patricia Field; and hair stylist Orlando Peter. A special Barbie produced for the campaign and sporting reproductions of fashion and styling from 1960's commercials and advertising was successful in attracting the younger generation to the campaign.

配布対象：プレゼントキャンペーン応募者　狙い・効果：販売促進
Target market : People requesting the campaign gifts
Aim and effect : Promoting sales

CL：プロクター・アンド・ギャンブル・ファー・イースト・インク　Prokter &
Gamble Far East, Inc.　CD, Planning：佐藤秀一　Hidekazu Sato
AD：清水克弘　Katsuhiro Shimizu　P（Barbie）：中瀬古雷太　Raita Nakaseko
P（Person）：内田将二　Shoji Uchida
Agency, SB：ビーコン コミュニケーションズ　beacon communications k.k.　Japan

ポップ　P.O.P

交通広告　Traffic AD

アナ スイ コスメティックス
商品購入者対象 プレゼントキャンペーン

Anna Sui Cosmetics Gift Campaign for customers

化粧品 Cosmetics

「アナ スイ コスメティックス」の商品を税込み5,250円以上購入すると非売品の
ノベルティグッズがもらえるプレゼントキャンペーンのために製作された、オリ
ジナルのカゴ。全国のコスメカウンターで配布された。配色はブラックで統一、
カゴ全体に同ブランドのシグニチャーである「ローズ」と「バタフライ」をあしらっ
たアナ スイ独特のデコラティブなデザインに仕上っている。

An original Anna Sui gift basket not available for purchase, produced for
the gift campaign and presented to customers who purchase Anna Sui
Cosmetics products to the value of ¥5,250 or more (tax included). The gift
baskets were distributed at Anna Sui Cosmetics stores throughout Japan.
The color scheme was consolidated with the color black and the entire gift
basket finished with Anna Sui's unique decorative design of roses and but-
terflies for which she is known.

配布対象：アナ スイ コスメティックスの商品購入者　配布方法・場所：全国のコスメカウ
ンター　制作数：20,000個　狙い・効果：新規購買者の獲得・来店促進
Target market : Purchasers of Anna Sui Cosmetics
Distribution method and area : Anna Sui Stores throughout Japan
Number produced : 20,000　**Aim and effect :** To attract new customers, promote
store traffic.

CL：アナ スイ コスメティックス　ANNA SUI COSMETICS
CD：アナ スイ　ANNA SUI　Package Design＝中野 恵　Megumi Nakano
SB：アルビオン　ALBION Co., Ltd.　Japan

アナ スイ コスメティックス / ポール＆ジョー
パーティ インビテーション

Anna Sui Cosmetics / Paul & Joe party invitation

化粧品 Cosmetics

二つのコスメブランドの2007年秋、新商品発表パーティのインビテーション。「艶めく
大人の女性達はゴージャスにおおはしゃぎ！」というコンセプトにふさわしく、パーティ
会場ではメイクはもちろん、ダーツとビリヤードも楽しめる。高級感のあるボックスを
開くと、中からオリジナルのダーツとビリヤードチョークが現れ、パーティへの好奇心
を高めるインビテーションとなっている。

An invitation for a party to announce the autumn 2007 new product lines of two
famous brands. Appropriately for the concept of "sexy women in gorgeously
high spirits," party guests enjoyed the make-up naturally, but also the darts and
billiards at the party venue. Inside the high-quality box are original darts and billiards chalk, serving to increase curiosity about the party.

配布対象：マスコミ関係者　配布方法・場所：郵送　狙い・効果：新製品のイメージ伝達
Target market : Media and other related persons　**Distribution method and area :** Mail
Aim and effect : Conveying image of new product range

CL：アルビオン　ALBION Co., Ltd.　AD, D：相場将司　Masashi Aiba
DF, SB：ジェネラルイントウキョウ　General in Tokyo　Japan

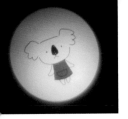

ライトキーホルダー
点灯するとコアラの絵柄
が映し出される。

Key ring with light
Turn the light on to see
the koala pattern.

ティナプリ「コアラのここらとコララ」キャンペーン

tina-pri "Kokora and Korara, the koalas" Campaign

美容 Cosmetics

おもてなしやサービスの象徴をキャラクター化し、社内教育用としてブランドブックを制作。絵本を読む感覚で企業理念を学ぶことのできるこの本は、リクルーティングや営業用ツールとしても広く活用された。同時期に作成されたストラップなどのノベルティは、機能性下着の無料試着体験をした客や営業用ツールとして配布され、ブランドの認知度やイメージアップに貢献した。

The koala characters were designed to symbolize hospitality and service and in a brand book produced for in-house training. The book in a picture-book style that teaches about the company's ideology was widely employed as a recruitment and business tool. Novelties such as the carry-strap produced around the same time were distributed to customers who took part in the free trial of the company's functional underwear line and as a tool for use in business, contributing to an increased recognition of the brand and enhancement of the brand's image.

配布対象：社員・試着体験をした来店者　配布方法・場所：ティナプリ全店
狙い・効果：来店者の増加とブランド認知度アップ
Target market : Company employees, customers who took part in the free trial　**Distribution method and area :** All tina-pri stores
Aim and effect : Increased customer numbers and increased brand awareness

CL：ティナプリ tina-pri　CD：伊藤敬生 Takao Ito
AD, D, I：常軒理恵子 Rieko Tsunenoki　D：今泉小夜 Sayo Imaizumi
CW：永野弥生 Yayoi Nagano　Novelty Planning：夏井英樹 Hideki Natsui
Agency, SB：電通九州 DENTSU KYUSHU INC.
DF：電通テック DENTSU TEC INC.　Japan

アナザーエディション 2008年
Spring & Summer プレビューノベルティ

Another Edition 2008 Spring / Summer Preview Novelty

アパレル Apparel

ユナイテッドアローズの展開するブランド、アナザーエディションが2008年のspring & summer用商品のプレビュー（シーズン到来の数ヶ月前に、雑誌編集者やスタイリストなどの業界関係者のみに商品を披露する展示会のこと）用に製作されたインビテーション・カードと、同時に配布されたノベルティグッズ。インビテーションは事前に郵送、グッズはプレビュー会場にて来場者に配布された。

Novelty goods distributed with the invitation card to the preview showing (a show that takes place a few months before the start of the season where the range is shown to people working in fashion-related fields such as magazine editors) of the 2008 spring/summer line by the Another Edition label, part of the major fashion label, United Arrows. The invitation was sent in advance of the show and the novelty goods were distributed at the preview venue.

配布対象：プレビュー来場者　配布方法・場所：プレビュー会場
狙い・効果：シーズンイメージの伝達
Target market : Guests at the preview showing
Distribution method and area : Preview venue
Aim and effect : Conveying the season's look

CL, SB：アナザーエディション Another Edition　Japan

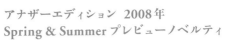

DM

アナザーエディション
新店舗案内用ステッカー

Another Edition New Store Information Stickers

アパレル Apparel

ユナイテッドアローズの展開するブランド、アナザーエディションの大阪・心斎橋店オープン後に製作した店舗案内。表面に「豚」、裏面は「ゼブラ」柄を印刷し、手にした後にすぐ捨てられてしまうことなく、長い間多くの人の目に触れられるようにするための工夫として、「シール」という形態を採用した。このシールは店内ラックに設置した他、店舗近隣のカフェなどに配布した。

Store information produced after the opening of the Shinsai-bashi, Osaka store of the Another Edition line, part of the major fashion label, United Arrows. Printed with a pig pattern on the front and a zebra pattern on the back, the sticker format was chosen as a device to make customers less inclined to throw the stickers away as soon as they receive them and to be an object of attention of as many people as possible over a long period of time. The stickers have been placed in racks around the store as well as distributed in cafes in the vicinity of the store.

配布方法・場所：館内ラック・近隣のカフェなど
Distribution method and area : In-store racks, nearby cafes etc.

CL, SB：アナザーエディション Another Edition　Japan

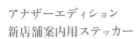

DM

アナザーエディション
2008年 Fall & Winter プレビューノベルティ
Another Edition 2008 Fall / Winter Preview Novelty Item

アパレル Apparel

ユナイテッドアローズの展開するブランド、アナザーエディションが2008年のfall & winter商品のプレビュー用に製作したインビテーション・カードと、会場で配布されたノベルティグッズ。インビテーションは「グリム童話」を、ノベルティはマカダミアナッツと唇型ブローチをつなげたブレスレットで、「シュール」と「農婦」をイメージしている。

The invitation card produced by the Another Edition line, part of the major fashion label, United Arrows, for the preview showing of its 2008 Fall / Winter line and the novelty item distributed at the preview venue. The design of the invitation was based on Grimms' fairytales and the novelty item, a bracelet decorated with macadamia nuts and a brooch in the shape of ips, conveyed the ideas of "surreal" and "farmer's wife".

配布対象：プレビュー来場者 **配布方法・場所**：プレビュー会場 **狙い・効果**：シーズンイメージの伝達
Target market：Guests at the preview showing **Distribution method and area**：Preview venue **Aim and effect**：Conveying the season's look

CL, SB：アナザーエディション Another Edition D：野川はるか Haruka Nogawa Japan

アナザーエディション
福岡店・町田店 オープンノベルティ
Another Edition :
Fukuoka and Machida store openings novelty

アパレル Apparel

ユナイテッドアローズの展開するブランド、アナザーエディションの福岡店と町田店のオープン記念として先着1000名ずつ配布したノベルティ。円型の缶にはコーン型のお香が封入されている。また、缶のデザインは、それぞれのお店の内装コンセプトを踏襲したデザインとなっている。

A novelty, a cone-shaped bottle of perfume packaged in a circular tin, distributed to the first 1,000 customers of the Another Edition fashion line, part of the major fashion label, United Arrows to mark the opening of the Fukuoka and Machida stores. The tin was designed to incorporate the concepts of the interior of each store.

配布対象：先着1,000名　配布方法・場所：店頭　狙い・効果：来店促進
Target market : First 1,000 customers
Distribution method and area : Stores
Aim and effect : Promote store traffic

CL, SB：アナザーエディション　Another Edition
AD：森 由美　Yumi Mori　Japan

アナザーエディション 新宿フラッグス店
リニューアル & 5th 記念ノベルティ

Another Edition Shinjuku Flags store : Reopening after renovation and fifth anniversary

アパレル Apparel

ユナイテッドアローズの展開するブランド、アナザーエディションの新宿フラッグス店5周年記念とリニューアルオープンを兼ねたノベルティ。高級バッグをイメージしたケースの中には、エッフェル塔をモチーフにしたオリジナルデザインのストラップが入っている。店頭の商品を1万円以上購入したお客様に配布。

A novelty produced to mark both the fifth anniversary of the Shinjuku Flags store of Another Edition, a United Arrows fashion brand, and the store's reopening after its renovation. With the themes of high-class handbag contains an original design carry-strap with a motif of the Eiffel Tower. The novelty is distributed to customers who purchase products to the value of ￥10,000 yen or more.

配布対象：商品購買者　配布方法・場所：店頭　狙い・効果：来店促進
Target market : Customers of Another Edition clothing　**Distribution method and area :** Stores
Aim and effect : Increase store foot traffic

CL, SB：アナザーエディション　Another Edition　AD：森 由美　Yumi Mori　Japan

MÅRCOMONDE 店頭ツール
MÅRCOMONDE : Store tools

アパレル Apparel

靴下ブランドMÅRCOMONDE（マルコモンド）は、シーズンごとに一つの国の一つの時代をテーマとして、その国を旅している気分になれるアイテムを提案している。定期的に青山のスパイラルにて開催される期間限定ショップ「Bazaar by MÅRCOMONDE」では、限定のショッパーを使用。クリスマスには、商品購入者にお菓子が詰め込まれたミニ靴下がプレゼントされる。

Socks brand MÅRCOMONDE, which features a new theme each season of a particular period in time in a particular country, offers a range of products that make you feel as if you are traveling in that country. Limited edition shoppers are used in the Bazaar store that is opened regularly for a limited period in Aoyama Spiral. Customers of MÅRCOMONDE products are presented with a pair of mini-socks filled with sweets.

配布対象：商品購入者　配布方法・場所：店頭
Target market : Customers of MÅRCOMONDE
Distribution method and area : Stores

CL, SB：ドロワー　DRAWER inc.
CD：角末有沙　Arisa Kakusue
AD, D：池田充宏　Mitsuhiro Ikeda　Japan

DM

DM

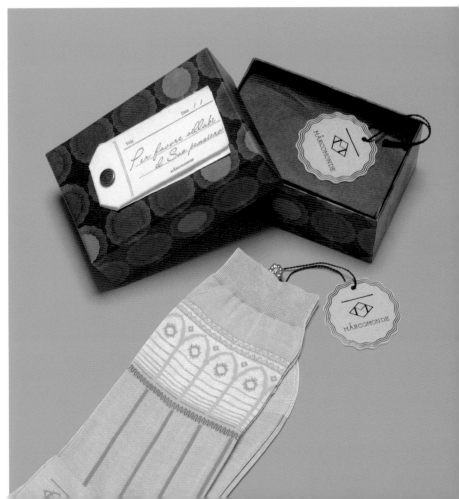

Pinceau 2008年 Autumn & Winter カタログ

Pinceau: 2008 Autumn / Winter Catalogue

アパレル Apparel

2008年A / Wのカタログのテーマは、「DIAMOND CAMP」。中央の見開きにはダイヤモンド型の切り込みを施し、巻末にはペーパーダイヤモンドのおまけを付けるなど、楽しい仕掛けを盛り込んだカタログに仕上げた。

The theme of the 2008 Autumn / Winter catalogue was "Diamond Camp." Diamond-shaped cuts in the center spread and paper diamond freebies at the back produced a catalogue full of fun and interesting devices.

配布対象：顧客 狙い・効果：シーズンイメージの伝達
Target market : Customers **Aim and effect :** Communication of the season's image

CL：ジュン Jun Co., Ltd. AD, D：平林奈緒美 Naomi Hirabayashi
D：米山菜津子 Natsuko Yoneyama P：田辺わかな Wakana Tanabe
DF, SB：プラグイングラフィック Plug-in Graphic Japan

Pinceau 2008年
Spring & Summer カタログ

Pinceau: 2008 Spring / Summer Catalogue

アパレル Apparel

新しく生まれてくるものと古き良きものを融合させ、こだわりと華や
かさをもった大人の女性に向けた服を提案しているPinceau。2008年
S/Sのカタログは、レコードジャケットのような正方形の仕様とし、古い
風合いを出すため、角にシワや汚れのデザインを施している。通常のカ
タログページ以外に、ポストカード式のものを同封し、特別感を高めた。

Pinceau, offering clothing for discriminating, fashionable women
who combine the best of the old and the new. The 2008 Spring /
Summer catalogue has the same square shape as a record sleeve,
and to make it look old, fold lines and dirt were added to the corners.
In addition to the usual catalogue pages, post card-type pages were
also inserted to increase the sense of the special nature of the book.

配布対象：顧客　狙い・効果：シーズンイメージの伝達
Target market : Customers　**Aim and effect :** Communication of the season's image

CL：ジュン Jun Co., Ltd.　AD：平林奈緒美 Naomi Hirabayashi
D：米山菜津子 Natsuko Yoneyama　P：三部正博 Masahiro Sanbe
DF, SB：プラグイングラフィック Plug-in Graphic　Japan

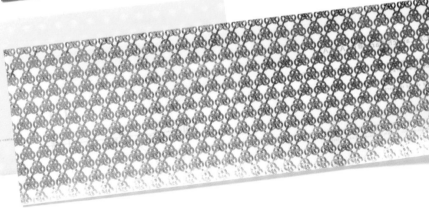

ARICA オープンノベルティ

ARICA : Opening novelty

アパレル Apparel

日本のファッションと文化を世界中の人々に発信するオンラインメディア「ARICA」。この誕生を記念したレセプションパーティにて、日本の代表的な工芸品である扇子や手ぬぐいが来場者にプレゼントされた。案内状も、金と赤をキーカラーとした和のデザインに仕上がっている。

Web-based media, ARICA, delivering Japanese fashion and culture to people around the world. At the reception commemorating its launch, a folding fan and a towel, both typical Japanese industrial art objects, were presented to guests. The invitation was in a Japanese design with key colors of gold and red.

配布対象：マスコミ関係者
配布方法・場所：[a]郵送・[b]レセプションパーティ会場
Target market : Media-related persons
Distribution method and area : [a]Mail・[b]Reception venue

CL：ARICA Inc.   AD, D：相羽将司 Masashi Aiba
DF, SB：ジェネラルイントウキョウ General in Tokyo   Japan

DM (a)

b

c

オンワード樫山「自由区」カレンダー
Onward Kashiyama "Area Free" calendar

アパレル Apparel

ファッションブランド「自由区」の顧客向けに配られているカレンダー。各月のイラストの一部に金と銀の箔押しが施されており、ケースの上部から日付が見える仕組みになっている。ブランドイメージ同様、大人の女性に向けた上品なデザインで、日常に溶け込む"ちょっと良いもの"を目指して製作された。

A calendar distributed to customers of the fashion brand, Area Free. A part of each month's illustration has undergone a gold and silver foiling process so that the date is visible through the top of the case. Similarly to the brand's image, the calendar has an elegant design that is targeted at women, the intention being "something of rather good quality" that becomes part of their everyday lives.

配布対象：「自由区」の顧客　配布方法・場所：各店舗
Target market : Area Free customers
Distribution method and area : All stores

CL：オンワード樫山　Onward Kashiyama Co., Ltd.
AD：鷲見 陽　Akira Sumi　D：内藤麻美子　Mamiko Naito
DF, SB：アンテナグラフィックベース　ANTENNA GRAPHIC BASE Co., Ltd
Japan

ドレス キャンプ 顧客限定
受注会のお土産
Gift campaign limited to DRESSCAMP customers

アパレル Apparel

2003年S/S東京コレクションでデビューして以来、高く評価されているブランド、ドレスキャンプ。2008年よりヘッドデザイナーにマラヤン・ペジョスキーが就任し注目を集める。ブランドイメージ同様、ラグジュアリーなデザインに仕上げられているスワロフスキーのピンズが顧客にプレゼントされた。

DRESSCAMP, a brand that has been highly regarded since its debut with a spring / summer Tokyo collection in 2003 . The appointment in 2008 of Marjan Pejoski as head designer attracted a lot of notice. In a similar style to the brand image, Swarovski pins finished in a luxury design were presented to customers.

配布対象：顧客　配布方法・場所：店頭　狙い・効果：顧客への感謝の意と今後の来店促進。受注会後から店頭にて販売。人気商品のため、現在も継続販売中。
Target market : Customers **Distribution method and area :** Stores
Aim and effect : An expression of appreciation to customers and to increase store traffic for the future. After the party where customers placed advance orders for products, the pins went on sale in stores. As they turned out to be a highly popular item, they continue to be sold.

CL, SB：ドレス キャンプ DRESSCAMP　Japan

ARTS & SCIENCE ホリデーブック
ARTS & SCIENCE Holiday Book

アパレル Apparel

クリスマスのホリデーシーズンに向け、ARTS & SCIENCEと各ブランドが制作したオリジナルの品を紹介するカタログ。「特別の日のための特別な品」を紹介するブックであるため、赤のベロア地にゴールドの箔押しを施し、限定感のある装丁に仕上げた。

A look book to introduce original items produced by ARTS & SCIENCE and its brands for the Christmas holiday season. As it was a book to introduce "special goods for a special day", gold foil was used on a red velour fabric and the book finished with a binding that created a sense of its limited nature.

配布対象：顧客　狙い・効果：ブランドイメージの伝達
Target market : Customers **Aim and effect :** Communication of the brand's image

CL：アーツ アンド サイエンス ARTS & SCIENCE
AD, D：平林奈緒美 Naomi Hirabayashi　P：山口恵史 Satoshi Yamaguchi
DF, SB：プラグイングラフィック Plug-in Graphic　Japan

CAHIER Nº4

MÄR ENTERPRISE. / SPRING AND SUMMER 2008
MÄR ENTERPRISE. / Printemps and Ete 2008
100mm×150mm
(2000 Copies)

4 942857 131277   2008

© 2007 MÄR ENTERPRISE.CO.,L
Printd in Japan.

MÄR ENTERPRISE. / 2008 Printemp   te

MÄR ENTERPRISE 2008年
Spring & Summer カタログ

MÄR ENTERPRISE 2008 Spring / Summer Catalogue

アパレル Apparel

「その人にとって、その人の『STYLE』を作れる余白を残した服」を目指しているMÄR ENTERPRISE。2008年S/Sのカタログは、革の手帳のような質感とサイズの仕様とし、MÄR ENTERPRISEの服のインスピレーションの源、素材、でき上がる工程を写真とイラストで表現した。

MÄR ENTERPRISE whose aim is "clothing where style is created by what you leave out." The 2008 Spring / Summer catalgue is designed in terms of texture and size to resemble a leather notebook, and the inspiration for MÄR ENTERPRISE clothes, the materials and the processes to make them have been expressed using photographs and illustrations.

配布対象：顧客 **狙い・効果**：シーズンイメージの伝達
Target market：Customers
Aim and effect：Communication of the season's image

CL：メーア エンタープライズ MÄR ENTERPRISE CO, LTD.
AD, D,P：平林奈緒美 Naomi Hirabayashi P：小野純子 Junko Ono
DF, SB：プラグイングラフィック Plug-in Graphic Japan

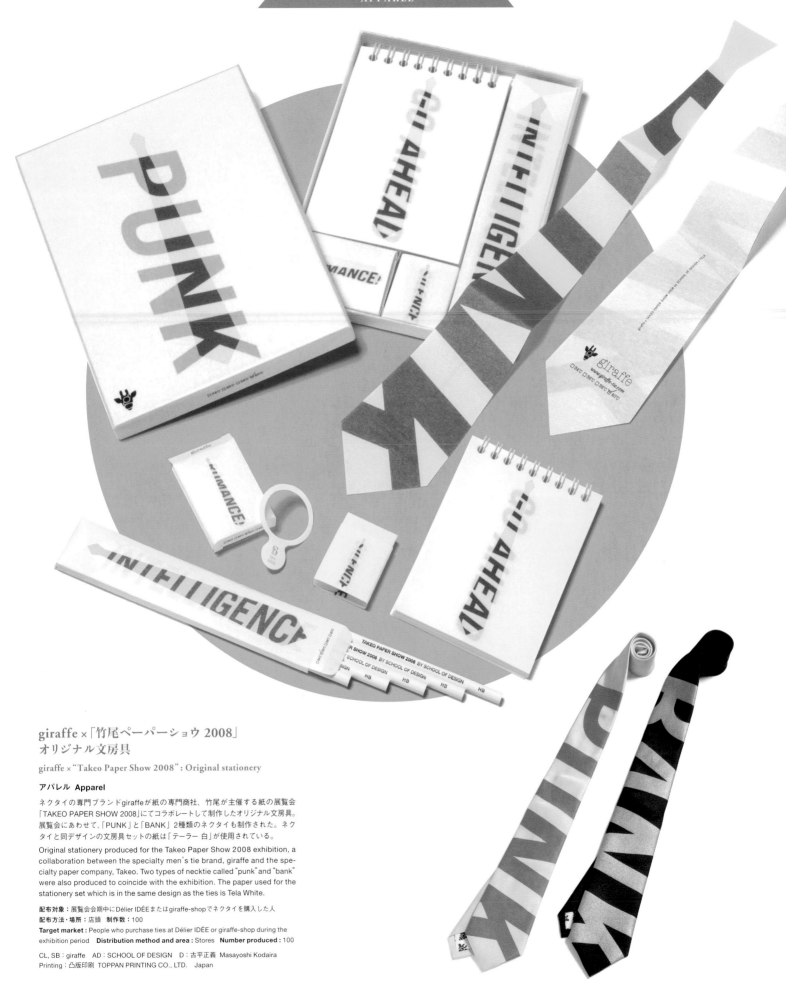

giraffe ×「竹尾ペーパーショウ 2008」
オリジナル文房具

giraffe × "Takeo Paper Show 2008" : Original stationery

アパレル Apparel

ネクタイの専門ブランドgiraffeが紙の専門商社、竹尾が主催する紙の展覧会「TAKEO PAPER SHOW 2008」にてコラボレートして制作したオリジナル文房具。展覧会にあわせて、「PUNK」と「BANK」2種類のネクタイも制作された。ネクタイと同デザインの文房具セットの紙は「テーラー 白」が使用されている。

Original stationery produced for the Takeo Paper Show 2008 exhibition, a collaboration between the specialty men's tie brand, giraffe and the specialty paper company, Takeo. Two types of necktie called "punk" and "bank" were also produced to coincide with the exhibition. The paper used for the stationery set which is in the same design as the ties is Tela White.

配布対象：展覧会会期中にDélier IDÉEまたはgiraffe-shopでネクタイを購入した人
配布方法・場所：店頭　制作数：100
Target market : People who purchase ties at Délier IDÉE or giraffe-shop during the exhibition period　**Distribution method and area :** Stores　**Number produced :** 100

CL, SB：giraffe　AD：SCHOOL OF DESIGN　D：古平正義　Masayoshi Kodaira
Printing：凸版印刷　TOPPAN PRINTING CO., LTD.　Japan

TAKEO KIKUCHI 店頭ツール Takeo Kikuchi : Store tools

アパレル Apparel

クリスマス、バレンタインなど特別なシーズンにのみ制作される期間限定ショッパー。表裏でデザインが異なるビニールカバーを通常のショッパーに被せる仕組みとなっており、それぞれがウィットに富んだデザインとなっている。

A limited edition shopper produced only for special seasons such as Christmas and Valentine's Day. The everyday shoppers are covered with vinyl covers that have different patterns on the front and the back. A clever idea.

配布対象：商品購入者　配布方法・場所：店頭　狙い・効果：来店促進・顧客の獲得
Target market : Customers of Takeo Kikuchi products　**Distribution method and area :** Stores
Aim and effect : Increase store traffic, attract new customers

CL：ワールド WORLD CO., LTD.　AD, D：相場将司 Masashi Aiba
DF, SB：ジェネラルイントウキョウ General in Tokyo　Japan

JEANASiS 店頭プレゼントキャンペーン JEANASiS : Store gift campaign

アパレル Apparel

JEANASiSのショップで商品購入者を対象に行われたプレゼントキャンペーン。パープルとライトグレーのストライプ柄の折り畳み傘は、ロゴは極力小さく入れ、はじめからデイリーで使えるものを目指して制作した。

A gift campaign for customers at JEANASiS stores. The novelty was a folding umbrella in a pattern of purple and light grey stripes, fun at the same time as being practical.

配布対象：商品購入者　配布方法・場所：店頭　狙い・効果：来店促進・顧客の獲得
Target market : Customers of JEANASiS products　**Distribution method and area :** Stores
Aim and effect : Increase store traffic, attract new customers

CL：ジーナシス JEANASiS.　AD, D：相場将司 Masashi Aiba　DF, SB：ジェネラルイントウキョウ General in Tokyo
Japan

Baby Beat 店頭販促ツール　Baby Beat : Store marketing tools

アパレル　Apparel

Baby Beatの商品購入者へのノベルティとして製作された、鏡とビニールバッグ。鏡が入っている組箱部分は取り外して、二次使用できる仕組みになっている。ビニールバッグはブランドロゴを象った絵柄で、黒を基調としたシックなデザインに仕上げた。

The novelty mirror and plastic bag produced for purchasers of Baby Beat products. Remove the inner box part that contains the mirror and apply it to another use. The plastic bag has a chic design in a pattern based on the brand logo on a base of black.

配布対象：Baby Beat商品購入者　配布方法・場所：店頭　制作数：600個
Target market : Baby Beat product purchasers　**Distribution method and area :** Stores
Number produced : 600

CL：ルック　LOOK Inc.　　AD, D：澤田千尋　Chihiro Sawada
DF, SB：アンテナグラフィックベース　ANTENNA GRAPHIC BASE Co., Ltd　Japan

Vol 1

And A 店頭配布アートフリーペーパー 「wall on」

And A : "wall on" novelty for store distribution

アパレル Apparel

ファッションのみならずアート・カルチャーの新しいスタイルやメッセージの発信として、2005年よりスタートしたアートフリーペーパー wall on（ウォール・オン）。Vol 1 はB4サイズのカレンダー、Vol 2 は便箋やメッセージカードとして使用できる仕様に、Vol 3 は家の中にあると楽しくなるコースター。各年、形が決まっていること以外は、アーティストが自由に制作している。

"wall on", an art free paper launched in 2005 to report not only new fashion styles and fashion news but also art culture. Volume 1 of the paper was in a B4-size calendar format, Volume 2 in a writing paper or message card format, and Volume 3,as fun coasters to use at home. Each year, the form of the novelty is decided and the artists then given free rein to come up with ideas.

配布対象：And A, And Accessoire, And A Hommeの全店
配布方法・場所：And A全店　**狙い・効果**：アートの発信
Target market：Visitors to the store
Distribution method and area：All And A stores,
And Accessoire, And A Homme
Aim and effect：Disseminating art culture

CL, SB：アンド エー　And A
Printing：テンプリント TENPRINT
Japan

Vol 2

Vol 3

And A 店頭配布フリーペーパー
And A free paper for store distribution

アパレル Apparel

AからZまで、各ページを様々なアーティストが自由にデザインしているフリーペーパー。「wall on」同様、個性豊かなラインナップに。numero1は、エコバッグに入れて配布された。

A free paper, each page of which going from A-Z is designed by various artists. Like "wall on," the lineup is full of originality. numero 1 is put into an original eco-bag to create a fun distribution method.

配布対象：1万円以上の商品購入者
配布方法・場所：And A, And Accessoire, And A Homme の全店　狙い・効果：カルチャーの発信
Target market : Purchasers of products to the value or ¥10,000 or more　**Distribution method and area :** All And A stores, And Accessoire, And A Homme
Aim and effect : Disseminating culture

CL, SB：アンド エー　And A
CD：アニエス・シュムトフ　Agnes Chemetoff
Printing：テンプリント　TENPRINT　Japan

LOWRYS FARM 店頭ツール
LOWRYS FARM : In-store promotional tools

アパレル Apparel

「女の子にとってシンプルに今の気分を楽しめる」をコンセプトとして掲げるLOWRYS FARM。シーズンや新店舗オープンごとに、通常バッグとはデザインが異なるショッパーを製作している。店舗ごとにポケットの色を変えたり、素材にこだわるなど、特別感があり日常的に使えるデザインとなっている。

Lowrys Farm with its concept of "Girls should simply enjoy the spirit of the moment." For each season and new store openings, Lowrys Farm usually produces a shopping bag that has a different design from ordinary bags. The bag has special features including a differently colored pocket for each store and a special attention to the materials used. The design means the bag can be used for other purposes.

配布対象：商品購入者 配布方法・場所：店頭 制作数：8,000 ～ 10,000個
狙い・効果：日常的に使ってもらうことで、広告としての役割も果たしている
制作コスト：単価250～500円
Target market : Purchasers of LOWRYS FARM products
Distribution method and area : Stores **Number produced :** 8,000-10,000 **Aim and effect :** The bag becomes an advertising medium when customers use the bag for other purposes. **Production costs :** ¥250-500

CL：ポイント Point Inc. AD, D：青木康子 Yasuko Aoki
DF, SB：パンゲア PANGEA Ltd.
Processing：ザ・パック The Pack Corporation Japan

apart by lowrys 店頭ツール
apart by lowrys : In-store promotional tools

アパレル Apparel

ブランドマークである「カギ」のモチーフを中心に、大人のかわいらしさを
強調したデザインとなっている。フリルのついたものなど、シーズンごと
にデザインの異なるショッパーを作るとともに、チロルチョコや金太郎飴
など、女の子が喜ぶお土産も製作した。

Based on the motif of a key that is the brand mark, the design empha-
sizes what's great about being a grown-up. As well the shopping bag
that comes in a different design each season, Tirol chocolates and
Kintaro hard candies were produced to delight the female customers.

配布対象：商品購入者　配布方法・場所：店頭　制作数：10,000～30,000個
狙い・効果：日常的に使ってもらうことで、広告としての役割も果たしている
制作コスト：単価25～350円
Target market : Purchasers of apart by lowrys products
Distribution method and area : Stores　**Number produced :** 10,000 – 30,000
Aim and effect : The bag becomes an advertising medium when customers use
the bag for other purposes.　**Production costs :** ¥25 – 350

CL：ポイント　Point Inc.　AD, D：青木康子　Yasuko Aoki
DF, SB：パンゲア　PANGEA Ltd.　Processing：ザ・パック　The Pack Corporation /
金太郎飴本店　Kintaro-Ame Honten / チロルチョコ　TIROL-CHOCO CO., LTD.
Japan

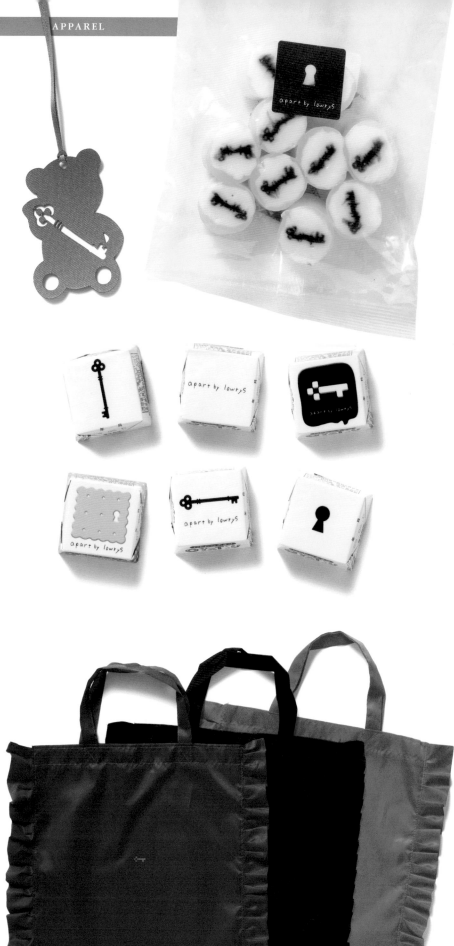

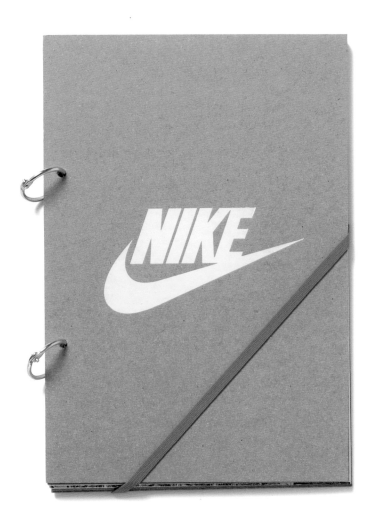

Nike 2005 年 Spring ルックブック　Nike : "2005 Spring Look Book"

スポーツ用品 Sporting goods

2005年 Spring のビジュアルテーマが「キャンパス」であることから、学校を連想するビジュアルをもとに、ルックブックを作成。1980年代のアメリカの学生が持っているようなゴムバンド付きのリングノートを使用した。ミニサイズ版は、クラブイベントで配布。持って帰りやすいサイズにすること、カラーバリエーションを作ることで、集めるおもしろさも狙った。巻末にはステッカーもついている。

Because the visual theme for spring 2005 was "campus," the Look Book was produced on the basis of visuals associated with school. The exercise books held together with an elastic band carried by American students in the 1980s were produced. The mini version was distributed at club events. The aim was to have fun collecting the exercise books by producing them in various easy-to-carry sizes and different colors. Stickers were also included in the back of the books.

配布対象：マスコミ関係者・イベント来場者　配布方法・場所：郵送・イベント会場で配布
狙い・効果：シーズンイメージの伝達
Target market : Media-related persons, visitors to events　**Distribution method and area :** Distributed by mail and at event venues　**Aim and effect :** Communication of the season's look

CL：ナイキジャパン　NIKE Japan　AD, D：小宮山秀明　Hideaki Komiyama　DF, SB：TGB design.　Japan

Nike Women 2005 年 Spring ルックブック
Nike Women : "2005 Spring Look Book"

スポーツ用品 Sporting goods

スポーツを連想させ、より強いインパクトを与えるため、リストバンドのような
ブックケースに入れて郵送されたルックブック。その年に発売されたリストバン
ド型の時計がアイデアのもととなっている。ターゲットである女性を意識し、フェ
ミニンなデザインに仕上げられた。

A Look Book mailed out in packaging that resembled a wristband, so as to
make the connection with sport and for a stronger impact. The basis for the
idea was the wristband-shaped watch released that year. The design was
feminine showing an awareness of the female target market.

配布対象：マスコミ関係者　配布方法・場所：郵送　狙い・効果：シーズンイメージの伝達
Target market : Media-related persons　**Distribution method and area :** Mail
Aim and effect : Communication of the season's look

CL：ナイキジャパン　NIKE Japan　AD, D：小宮山秀明　Hideaki Komiyama
DF, SB：TGB design.　Japan

Air Zoom Brave 2

軽快なプレースタイルで知られる田臥選手はコートオン・オフのシューズにも最大限にこだわっている。このシューズには、より俊敏な動きにこだわりを持ち、美しい横方向の俊敏な動きを可能にするバスケットボールシューズを作った。クイックステップのためのサイドからのサポート、そして軽快にするズームエアを装着。田臥選手をお気に入りのブルーを含めた色をHolidayに展開。

For his quick style of play, Yuta Tabuse has his footwear specific to his performance basketball "kodawari" for his footwear: on and off court. Working one on one with Nike designers, Yuta helped us create a high performance Nike Zoom Air, lateral forefoot support, and an outsole for quick step work and grips. 3 color ways including blue — Yuta's favorite — will be available starting this holiday.

Nike「Tokyo Design Studio」
案内状&ノベルティ

Nike : "Tokyo Design Studio" invitation and novelty

スポーツ用品 Sporting goods

「Tokyo Design Studio (TDS)」のオープンを記念したレセプションの案内状と来場者に配られたノベルティ。Nikeのデザインは、全てスケッチから生み出されたという想いから、来場者へのお土産として鉛筆とノートのセットが渡された。案内状はスタジオの場所がポップアップで記されており、持ち歩きやすいよう、情報が記されたカードも同封されている。

An invitation to the reception commemorating the opening of Tokyo Design Studio (TDS) and a novelty distributed to guests. Based on the idea that Nike designs are produced entirely from sketches, a pencil and notebook set were handed out to guests as souvenirs. The invitation showed the TDS location in pop-up format, and an easy-to-carry card containing information was also enclosed.

配布対象：マスコミ関係者 配布方法・場所：レセプションで配布
Target market : Media-related persons
Distribution method and area : Distributed at the reception

CL：ナイキジャパン NIKE Japan   AD, D：小宮山秀明 Hideaki Komiyama
DF, SB：TGB design.   Japan

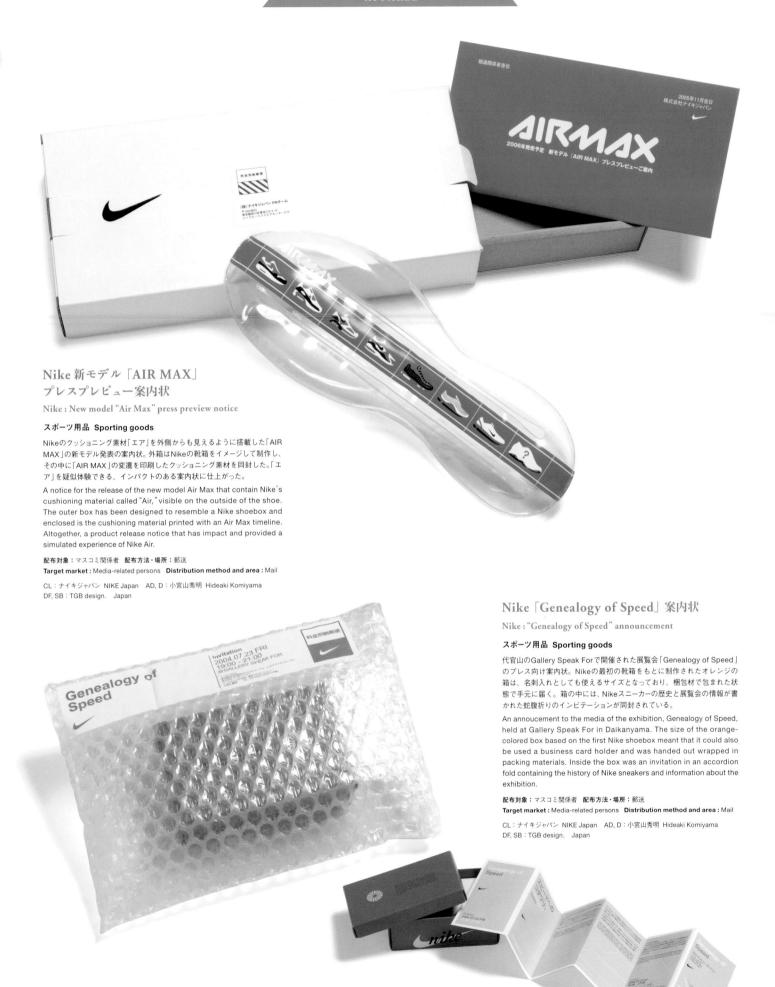

Nike 新モデル「AIR MAX」
プレスプレビュー案内状

Nike : New model "Air Max" press preview notice

スポーツ用品 Sporting goods

Nikeのクッショニング素材「エア」を外側からも見えるように搭載した「AIR MAX」の新モデル発表の案内状。外箱はNikeの靴箱をイメージして制作し、その中に「AIR MAX」の変遷を印刷したクッショニング素材を同封した。「エア」を疑似体験できる、インパクトのある案内状に仕上がった。

A notice for the release of the new model Air Max that contain Nike's cushioning material called "Air," visible on the outside of the shoe. The outer box has been designed to resemble a Nike shoebox and enclosed is the cushioning material printed with an Air Max timeline. Altogether, a product release notice that has impact and provided a simulated experience of Nike Air.

配布対象：マスコミ関係者　配布方法・場所：郵送
Target market : Media-related persons　**Distribution method and area** : Mail

CL：ナイキジャパン　NIKE Japan　AD, D：小宮山秀明　Hideaki Komiyama
DF, SB：TGB design.　Japan

Nike「Genealogy of Speed」案内状

Nike : "Genealogy of Speed" announcement

スポーツ用品 Sporting goods

代官山のGallery Speak Forで開催された展覧会「Genealogy of Speed」のプレス向け案内状。Nikeの最初の靴箱をもとに制作されたオレンジの箱は、名刺入れとしても使えるサイズとなっており、梱包材で包まれた状態で手元に届く。箱の中には、Nikeスニーカーの歴史と展覧会の情報が書かれた蛇腹折りのインビテーションが同封されている。

An annoucement to the media of the exhibition, Genealogy of Speed, held at Gallery Speak For in Daikanyama. The size of the orange-colored box based on the first Nike shoebox meant that it could also be used a business card holder and was handed out wrapped in packing materials. Inside the box was an invitation in an accordion fold containing the history of Nike sneakers and information about the exhibition.

配布対象：マスコミ関係者　配布方法・場所：郵送
Target market : Media-related persons　**Distribution method and area** : Mail

CL：ナイキジャパン　NIKE Japan　AD, D：小宮山秀明　Hideaki Komiyama
DF, SB：TGB design.　Japan

Nike「Air Force 1」
25周年イベント記念品

A party souvenir for "Nike Air Force 1"
turns 25 launching event

スポーツ用品 Sports goods

Nike「Air Force 1」の発売25周年イベントの記念品として制作された封かんセット。スタンプには、各VIPゲストのイニシャルを施している。イベントでは、このシューズの源となった音楽、ブレークダンス、ストリートカルチャーを振り返り、インスタレーションやモーショングラフィックス、ニューモデルと歴代AF1が展示された。

The party souvenir for Nike "Air Force 1" turns 25 launching event was a set of sealing stamp and wax. They were personalised for each VIP guest. In retrospect of AF1's origins, which are music, breakdance and street culture, the party exhibited interactive installations, motion graphics and a showcase of AF1 history in conjunction with the launch of new AF1 shoes.

CL：NIKE INC.　AD, SB：AllRightsReserved Ltd.
Hong Kong

SINCE 1982, AIR FORCE 1 IS A LANDMARK OF FINE HERITAGE IN SPORT, CULTURE AND BEYOND. LIKEWISE, THE DELICATE WAX SEAL HAS LONG BEEN THE CLASSIC HALLMARK OF FINESSE. THIS PREMIUM BOX SET IS BOTH AN EXCLUSIVE TOKEN OF AF1'S CRAFTSMANSHIP AND AN EXCEPTIONAL SOUVENIR OF THIS HISTORICAL "1 NIGHT".

25 YEARS OF UNDISPUTED LOVE
1 NIGHT OF CELEBRATION
JANUARY 6, 2007, 9:00 PM
CENTRAL STAR FERRY PIER NO.7
GENTLEMEN MUST WEAR SNEAKERS
INVITE ONLY, NON-TRANSFERABLE

R.S.V.P.
MARIA LEUNG
MARIA@ASIAN-VIBE.COM
852.3106.0492

Nike「Air Jordan 23」ワンナイトイベント記念品

An event souvenir for one-night concept night club of "Air Jordan 23"

スポーツ用品 Sporting goods

エアジョーダン23周年を記念した、一夜だけのコンセプト・ナイト・クラブがオープン。DJやダンスパフォーマンスが繰り広げられたこのイベントの記念品として、エアジョーダンのロゴをあしらったキャンパスリングなどのギフトを制作。ジョーダン23のコンセプト・ミュージアムはその後1ヶ月間開催された。

A campus ring was produced as the special gift for one-night concept night club of "Jordan 23", featuring the mega mascot of Jordan 23 anniversary edition, live DJing and dancing performance. Jordan 23 concept museum would last for 1 month for public.

CL：NIKE INC.　　AD, SB：AllRightsReserved. Ltd　Hong Kong

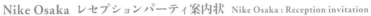

Nike Osaka　レセプションパーティ案内状　Nike Osaka : Reception invitation

スポーツ用品 Sporting goods

大阪初のフラッグショップ「Nike Osaka」オープンに伴うレセプションパーティの案内状。オリジナルのスニーカーをデザインできる「Nike iD」の引き換え券が入ったボックスは、ファッションカルチャーに強いプレスや関係者にのみ配られた。ボックスはテーマカラーである黒と銀を、カードは黒と金を使用した高級感溢れるデザインに仕上がっている。

An invitation to a reception for the opening of Osaka's Nike flagship store, Nike Osaka. The box containing the exchange vouchers for Nike iD, where you can make a pair of original Nikes in your own design, were distributed only to media and other persons with strong ties to fashion culture. Both exude a sense of high quality using the theme colors of black and silver for the box, black and gold for the card.

配布対象：マスコミ関係者　配布方法・場所：郵送
Target market : Media-related persons　**Distribution method and area :** Mail

CL：ナイキジャパン NIKE Japan　　AD, D：小宮山秀明 Hideaki Komiyama　　DF, SB：TGB design.　　Japan

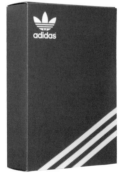

アディダス プロモーションツール
adidas : Promotional tool

スポーツ用品 Sporting goods

プレス関係者や顧客用に作られた、リラックスボーイフィギュア6体入りボックスセット。雑誌「relax」の中に登場するリラックスボーイの指人形が、アディダスの服を着ていたり、キャップをかぶっている。

A box set containing 6 Relax Boy figures created for media reps and customers. The Relax Boy finger puppets that appear in the magazine "relax" are wearing adidas clothing and caps.

配布対象：プレス関係者・顧客　制作数：約200個
Target market : Media-related persons, customers
Number produced : 200

CL：アディダス ジャパン / マガジンハウス　adidas Japan K.K /
Magazine House Ltd.　AD, D：石浦 克　Masaru Ishiura
DF, SB：TGB design.　Japan

アディダス
60周年記念フリーペーパー

The free paper "PAPER SKY × originals,"
a collaboration between the magazine and adidas

スポーツ用品 Sporting goods

60周年を迎えた「アディダス」と雑誌「PAPER SKY」とのコラボによって誕生したフリーペーパー「PAPER SKY × originals」。モデル写真のページでは59人のスタイリストが参加、読者のあなたが60番目のスタイリスト、というアディダス60周年にちなんだ企画となっている。

"PAPER SKY" and adidas which is celebrating its 60th anniversary. Fifty-nine stylists participated in the photography for the pages featuring models, and the reader was invited to become the "sixtieth" stylist as way of making an association with the sixtieth year of adidas.

配布対象：来店者　配布方法・場所：店頭
Target market : Visitors to the store　**Distribution method and area :** Stores

CL：アディダス ジャパン　adidas Japan K.K
AD：水野 学　Manabu Mizuno　D：仲山慎哉　Shinya Nakayama /
上村 昌　Masaru Uemura
DF, SB：グッドデザインカンパニー　good design company　Japan

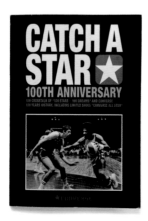

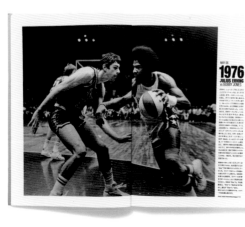

コンバース
「100th ANNIVERSARY SHOES IN BOOK」キャンペーン

Converse : "100th Anniversary Shoes In Book" campaign

スニーカー　Sneakers

コンバース生誕100周年を記念して製作された「100th ANNIVERSARY SHOES IN BOOK」。古い雑誌に見立てたダンボールの集合体の中に、シューズ（非売品のリニューアルスペック付キャンバスオールスター）を付録している。44枚の背表紙にヒストリートピックスを記載することで、100周年までの積み重ねを演出している。2007年3月より開設された特設サイトで、夢に向かって進む100名と夢を実現させた憧れの「Star」100名による対談を掲載。この内容がまとめられた1冊のBOOKが特典として同封されている。

This is produced in commemoration of the 100th anniversary of the founding of Converse. Specially redesigned canvas All Stars (not for general sale) have been inserted into a cardboard package made to look like a collection of magazines. The spines of all 44 books are inscribed with an historical topic of the past 100 years. The special web site set up since March 2007 features conversations with 100 people who are working towards achieving their dreams and 100 "stars" whose dreams have become reality.

配布対象：POPEYE、PS、WARP、JILLEなど雑誌媒体での読者プレゼント・シューズ購入者対象のコンバース店頭キャンペーン。青山ブックセンター、TSUTAYA TOKYO ROPPONGI、BEAMS、国立新美術館などで販売。　制作数：1,000個　狙い・効果：WEB上で展開してきた「catch a star 100 stars ×100 dreams」を形に残すものとして、ブックを製作。シューズ付きの形状とすることで、ブック自体が広告として機能することを狙った。

Target market : A gift for readers in the medium of a magazine (for example, Popeye, PS, Warp and Jille), Converse store campaign for customers of Converse shoes.
Number produced : 1,000　**Aim and effect :** "catch a star 100 stars × 100 dreams" that featured on the web site was produced as a book for the campaign. The aim was for the book to function as advertising by teaming it with the Converse shoes.

CL：コンバースジャパン　CONVERSE JAPAN CO., LTD.
AD：藤本やすし　Yasushi Fujimoto
Editorial Director：大山ゆかり（ロケットカンパニー）Yukari Oyama (Rocket Company)
Editor：工藤健士（ロケットカンパニー）Takeshi Kudo (Rocket Company) /
源 さち恵（ロケットカンパニー）Sachie Minamoto (Rocket Company)
D：中村有一朗　Yuichiro Nakamura
Agency, SB：オオツキプランニング　OTSUKI PLANNING INC.
Agency：コスモ・コミュニケーションズ　Cosmo Communications
DF：キャップ　CAP CO., LTD.　Printing：レーエ　re-e CO., LTD.　Japan

ポスター Poster

inhabitant.

www.inhabitant.jp

Inhabitant
「展示会 & MIXPRESSION 9
インハビタントブース」ノベルティグッズ
"Inhabitant Exhibition & MIXPRESSION 9
Inhabitant Booth" : Novelty goods

スノー・ストリートアパレル Snow street apparel

「MIXPRESSION 9」というメッセンジャー向けのイベントで配布されたノベルティグッズ。メッセンジャーたちに喜んでもらえるようにと作成されたスポークカードは、ブランドカラーのグリーンを基調としたものを中心に種類も豊富。それぞれのカードに入ったコピーは遊び心が感じられるものばかりで、それがそのまま「Inhabitant＝楽しい」というイメージに結びついている。

Novelty goods distributed at an event for MIXPRESSION 9 messengers. The brief was to produce something that would be popular among the messengers. The large variety of "spoke cards" produced are based on the green that is the brand's color. The copy that has been written for each card is fun and connects with the brand's image of "Inhabitant equals fun."

配布対象：展示会来場者・MIXPRESSION 9の大会参加者
配布方法・場所：展示会場・インハビタントブース　制作数：300個
狙い・効果：スポークカードだったため、メッセンジャーからの評判がよく、ブランドイメージの認知度がアップした　制作コスト：100,000円
Target market : Exhibition visitors and participants in the MIXPRESSION 9 competition
Distribution method and area : Exhibition venue, Inhabitant booths **Number produced :** 300 **Aim and effect :** The spoke cards were popular among the messengers and recognition of the brand image increased. **Production costs :** ¥100,000

CL：フェニックス phenix　CD, AD, CW：井上広一 Koichi Inoue
D：佐藤勝昭 Katsuaki Sato　P：水崎浩志 Hiroshi Mizusaki
DF, SB：オーイェル ORYEL　Japan

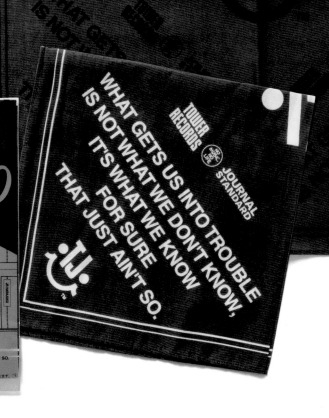

ジャーナルスタンダード表参道店 オープン ノベルティ
JOURNAL STANDARD Omotesando store : Opening novelty

アパレル Apparel

ジャーナルスタンダード表参道店のオープンに伴い作られた、告知用のミニフロシキとキャンドル。ミニフロシキは、オープン日が記載されたパッケージに封入され、街頭で配布された。商品購入者にプレゼントされたキャンドルは、紫と黄色の2色で、ラベンダーとグレープフルーツの香り。ブランド名が箔押しされた箱に入れてプレゼントされた。

A mini-furoshiki and candle produced to announce the opening of the JOURNAL STANDARD Omotesando store. The mini-furoshiki is wrapped in packaging inscribed with the date of the store opening and is distributed on the street. The purple and yellow candle presented to customers has a lavender and grapefruit fragrance and is placed in a box imprinted with the brand name in gold foil.

配布対象：商品購入者（キャンドルのみ）　配布方法・場所：店頭・街頭
制作数：[a] 2,000・[b] 300　狙い・効果：来店促進
Target market : Customers of JOURNAL STANDARD products (Only candles)
Distribution method and area : Stores, Street　**Number produced** : [a] 2,000・[b] 300
Aim and effect : Increase store traffic

CL, SB：JS. WORKS co., ltd. (BAYCREW'S GROUP)　D：山川伊久　Iku Yamakawa /
前定さおり　Saori Maesada / 原野 拓　Taku Harano (BAYCREW'S CREATIVE division)
Processing [a]：ザ・パック　THE PACK CORP.
Processing [b]：F・L・A・T　Japan

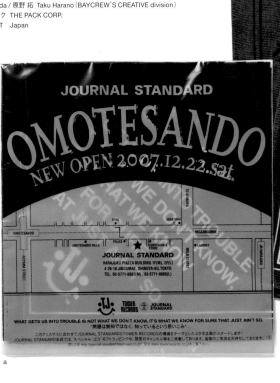

a

b

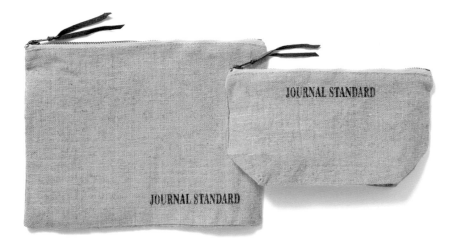

ジャーナルスタンダード大阪店
リニューアルオープン ノベルティ

JOURNAL STANDARD Osaka store :
Reopening after renovation novelty

アパレル Apparel

ジャーナルスタンダード大阪店リニューアルオープンの際に、商品購入者を
対象に配られたノベルティ。メンズはハンドタオル、歯ブラシなどが同封
されたトラベルセットを、レディースは麻のポーチ2個セットを製作した。

Novelties distributed to customers on the occasion of the reopening of the
JOURNAL STANDARD Osaka store after its renovation. The men's novelty is a
travel set that contains, among other things, a hand towel and a toothbrush; the
women's is a set of two linen pouches.

配布対象：商品購入者　配布方法・場所：店頭　狙い・効果：来店促進
Target market : Customers of JOURNAL STANDARD products
Distribution method and area : Stores　**Aim and effect :** Increase store traffic

CL, SB：JS. WORKS co., ltd.（BAYCREW'S GROUP）
CD, AD：BAYCREW'S CREATIVE division　D：前定さおり　Saori Maesada
Processing：トランス　TRANS co., ltd.　Japan

ジャーナルスタンダード堀江店
リニューアルオープン ノベルティ

JOURNAL STANDARD Horie store : Reopening after renovation novelty

アパレル Apparel

ジャーナルスタンダード堀江店のリニューアルオープンの際に、商品購入者にプレゼントさ
れた手帳。ウィンドウディスプレイと同じステッカーが貼られ、表紙にはロゴが入っている。

A notebook presented to customers on the occasion of the reopening of the
JOURNAL STANDARD Horie store after its renovation. The notebook is decorated
with the same stickers used for the window display and has the JOURNAL
STANDARD logo on the cover.

配布対象：商品購入者　配布方法・場所：店頭　制作数：300個　狙い・効果：来店促進
Target market : Customers of JOURNAL STANDARD products
Distribution method and area : Stores　**Number produced :** 300
Aim and effect : Increase store traffic

CL, SB：JS. WORKS co., ltd.（BAYCREW'S GROUP）　D：前定さおり　Saori Maesada /
原野 拓　Taku Harano（BAYCREW'S CREATIVE division）　Japan

スピック アンド スパン大阪ディアモール店　オープンノベルティ
Spick and Span : Osaka Diamor store : Opening novelty

アパレル　Apparel

スピックアンドスパン大阪ディアモール店オープンの際に、商品購入者にプレゼントされたショッパー。リボンやバッジがついた、女性に嬉しいデザインとなっている。

A shopping bag presented to purchasers of Spick and Span products on the occasion of the opening of its Osaka Diamor store. The novelty's design with its ribbon and badges was a hit with female customers.

配布対象：商品購入者　配布方法・場所：店頭　制作数：500枚　狙い・効果：来店促進
Target market : Customers of Spick and Span products　**Distribution method and area :** Stores
Number produced : 500　**Aim and effect :** Increase store traffic

CL, SB：FRAME WORKS co., ltd. (BAYCREW'S GROUP)　CD, D：BAYCREW'S CREATIVE division
Processing (Bag)：ザ・パック　THE PACK CORP.　Processing (Badge)：タイヨープラン　TAIYO PLAN., INC.
Japan

エディットフォールル西梅田店 オープンノベルティ
edit. for LuLu Nishi-Umeda store： Opening novelty

アパレル　Apparel

エディットアンドフォールル西梅田店オープンの際に、商品購入者にプレゼントされたシルクスカーフ。金色の箔押しが施された上品なケースにパープルのスカーフが入っており、こちらも金色の文字で「LULU」と記されている。

A silk scarf presented to customers of edit. for LuLu products on the occasion of the opening of the edit. for LuLu Nishi-Umeda store. Inside the sophisticated gold-foiled case is the purple scarf inscribed with the name LuLu in gold lettering.

配布対象：商品購入者　配布方法・場所：店頭
制作数：600セット　狙い・効果：来店促進
Target market : Customers of edit. for LuLu products
Distribution method and area : Stores
Number produced : 600　**Aim and effect :** Increase store traffic

CL, SB：JOINT WORKS CO., LTD.
CD, AD：BAYCREW'S CREATIVE division
D：福田十詩子 Toshiko Fukuda
　　（BAYCREW'S CREATIVE division）　Printing：TMK
Processing：フェアファクスコレクティブ　FAIRFAX COLLECTIVE
Japan

DEUXIÈME CLASSE 大阪店　リニューアルオープン ノベルティ
DEUXIÈME CLASSE Osaka store : Reopening after renovation novelty

アパレル　Apparel

DEUXIÈME CLASSE大阪店リニューアルの際に、商品購入者にプレゼントされたキャンドル。ブランドイメージと同様、高級感のあるシックなデザインとなっている。

A candle presented to customers on the occasion of the reopening of the DEUXIÈME CLASSE Osaka store after its renovation. Similarly to the brand's image, the novelty has a chic, high-quality design.

配布対象：商品購入者　配布方法・場所：店頭　制作数：450個　狙い・効果：来店促進
Target market : Customers of DEUXIÈME CLASSE products　**Distribution method and area :** Stores
Number produced : 450　**Aim and effect :** Increase store traffic

CL, SB：LE DOME CO., LTD. (BAYCREW'S GROUP)　CD, AD：BAYCREW'S CREATIVE division
D：福田十詩子 Toshiko Fukuda (BAYCREW'S CREATIVE division)　Printing：ザ・パック　THE PACK CORP.
Processing：美元堂 Bigendo / デニオ総合研究所 DENIAU Sogokenkyusho LTD.　Japan

gomme S/S、A/W 店頭販促ツール

gomme (spring / summer, autumn / winter collections) : Store marketing tools

アパレル Apparel

ファッションデザイナー・真木洋茂氏の手がけるブランド「gomme」が春夏、秋冬の新作立ち上げの際、直営店や卸店で商品を購入したお客様に配布したノベルティグッズ。ミネラルウォーター、キャンドル、タオルなど、各シーズンとも男女を問わず喜ばれるアイテムを選定している。

Novelty goods distributed to customers who purchased items at either gomme's own stores or wholesale stores from the new line released by fashion designer for the gomme brand, Hiroshige Maki for the spring / summer, autumn / winter seasons. The items chosen for each season were popular with both men and women alike and included mineral water, candles and towels.

配布対象：直営店・卸店の商品購入者　配布方法・場所：店頭
制作数：1,000個　狙い・効果：新作立ち上げの際の集客
制作コスト：500円
Target market : Customers who purchased products at gomme's own stores or wholesale stores
Distribution method and area : Stores　**Number produced :** 1,000
Aim and effect : Attracting customers for the new season's range
Production costs : ¥500

CL, SB：ゴム　gomme　D：真木洋茂　Hiroshige Maki　Japan

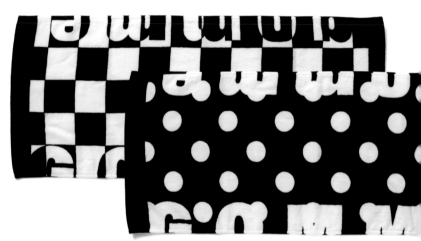

ÉDIFICE MATÉRIAUX 大阪店 オープン ノベルティ

ÉDIFICE MATÉRIAUX : Osaka store : Opening novelty

アパレル Apparel

現代の「COMFORT STYLE」を提案、発信するÉDIFICE MATÉRIAUXの大阪店オープンの際に作られたノベルティ。大人の男性が喜ぶ、ゴルフツールをプレゼントした。

A novelty created for the opening of the ÉDIFICE MATÉRIAUX Osaka store that offers modern, comfortable style.

配布対象：商品購入者　配布方法・場所：店頭　狙い・効果：来店促進
Target market : Customers of ÉDIFICE MATÉRIAUX products
Distribution method and area : Stores
Aim and effect : Increase store traffic

CL, SB：LE DOME CO., LTD. (BAYCREW'S GROUP)
CD, AD, D：BAYCREW'S CREATIVE division　Japan

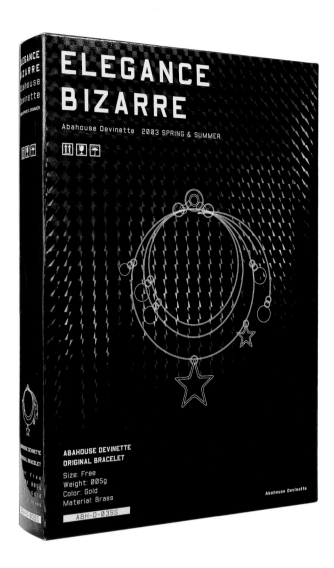

ELEGANCE
BIZARRE

Abahouse Devinette 2003 SPRING & SUMMER

ABAHOUSE DEVINETTE
ORIGINAL BRACELET

Size: Free
Weight: 005g
Color: Gold
Material: Brass

ABH-D-03SS

Abahouse Devinette

Abahouse Devinette

Abahouse Devinette
オリジナルブレスレット付 カタログ

Abahouse Devinette：Look Book with original gift

アパレル Apparel

媚びることのない意志を秘めた女性たちのために、軽妙で洒脱な開放されたスタイルを提案するブランド。限定感を高めるため、カタログとブレスレットがセットとなったオリジナルボックスを配布。カタログとボックスの表紙にはホログラムPPが施され、各ページは袋綴じとし、開くとスタイリングが見られる仕組みとした。

A brand offering a clever, unconventional and expansive style for women who refuse to play the coquette. To enhance the idea of its limited nature, the Look Book and an original bracelet were distributed as a set in an original box. A hologram PP was placed on the box and the cover of the Look Book, and each page bound with a covered binding so that the stylings emerge when the book is opened.

配布対象：顧客　**狙い・効果：**シーズンイメージの伝達
Target market：Customers
Aim and effect：Communication of the season's image

CL：アバハウスインターナショナル　Abahouse International Co.
AD, D：野尻大作　Daisaku Nojiri　DF, SB：ground　Japan

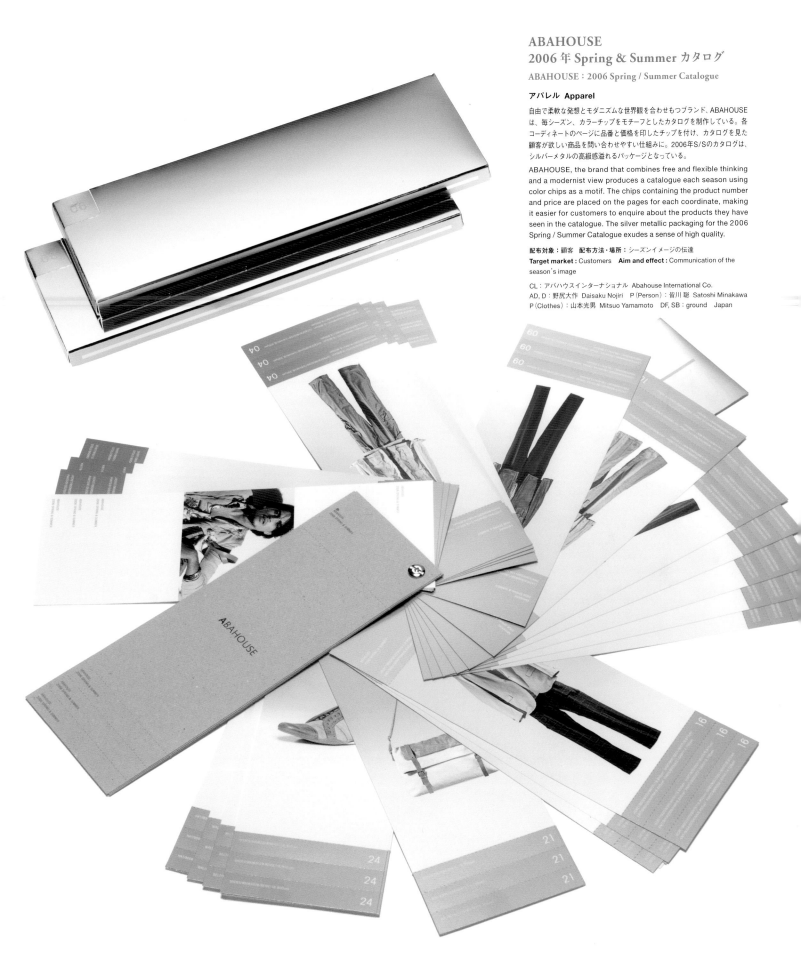

ABAHOUSE
2006 年 Spring & Summer カタログ
ABAHOUSE：2006 Spring / Summer Catalogue

アパレル Apparel

自由で柔軟な発想とモダニズムな世界観を合わせもつブランド、ABAHOUSE
は、毎シーズン、カラーチップをモチーフとしたカタログを制作している。各
コーディネートのページに品番と価格を印したチップを付け、カタログを見た
顧客が欲しい商品を問い合わせやすい仕組みに。2006年S/Sのカタログは、
シルバーメタルの高級感溢れるパッケージとなっている。

ABAHOUSE, the brand that combines free and flexible thinking
and a modernist view produces a catalogue each season using
color chips as a motif. The chips containing the product number
and price are placed on the pages for each coordinate, making
it easier for customers to enquire about the products they have
seen in the catalogue. The silver metallic packaging for the 2006
Spring / Summer Catalogue exudes a sense of high quality.

配布対象：顧客　配布方法・場所：シーズンイメージの伝達
Target market : Customers　**Aim and effect :** Communication of the
season's image

CL：アバハウスインターナショナル　Abahouse International Co.
AD, D：野尻大作　Daisaku Nojiri　P（Person）：皆川 聡　Satoshi Minakawa
P（Clothes）：山本光男　Mitsuo Yamamoto　DF, SB：ground　Japan

ABAHOUSE
2006年 Autumn & Winter
カタログ & ノベルティ
ABAHOUSE：
Autumn / Winter Catalogue and novelty

アパレル Apparel

2006年A/Wのカタログは、通常のものとアウターコレクションの2種類。ケースと表紙に印刷された木目の色を変え、差別化を図った。また、顧客へのノベルティとしてスカーフを制作。レコードジャケットほどの大きさのパッケージを開くと、中にはパッケージと同柄のスカーフが入っている。

Two versions of the 2006 Autumn / Winter Catalogue were produced : the regular catalogue and one for the outerwear collection. The catalogues were differentiated from each other by changing the grain printed on the case and the cover. A scarf was also produced as a novelty for customers. Open the packaging that is as large as a record sleeve to find inside a scarf in the same pattern as the packaging.

配布対象：顧客　狙い・効果：シーズンイメージの伝達
Target market : Customers **Aim and effect :** Communication of the season's image

CL：アバハウスインターナショナル　Abahouse International Co.
AD, D：野尻大作　Daisaku Nojiri
P（Person）：北井博也　Hiroya Kitai
P（Clothes）：樋口兼一　Kenichi Higuchi
DF, SB：ground　Japan

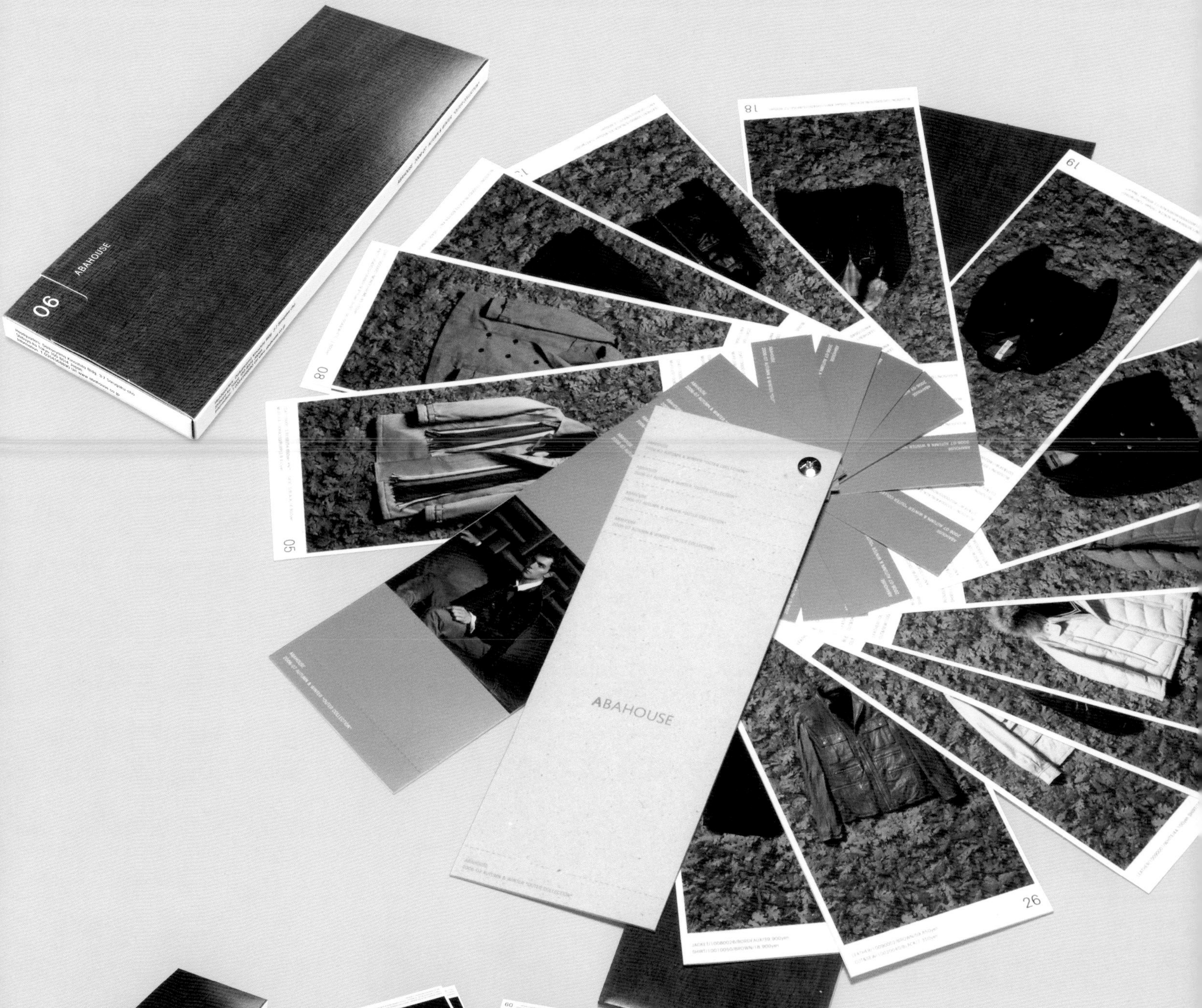
ABAHOUSE
06
ABAHOUSE
26

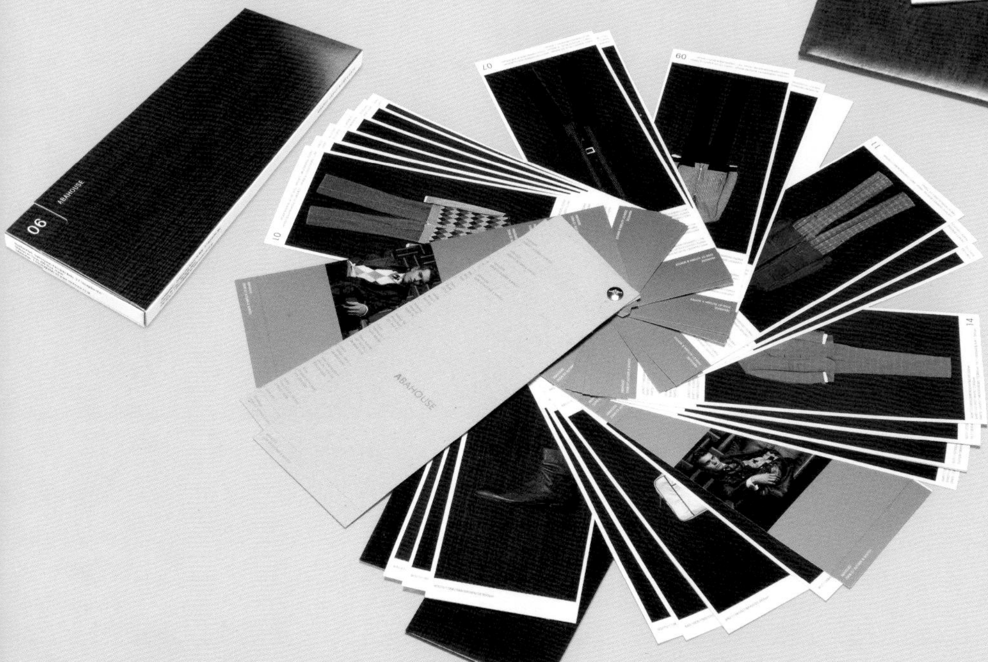
ABAHOUSE
06
ABAHOUSE

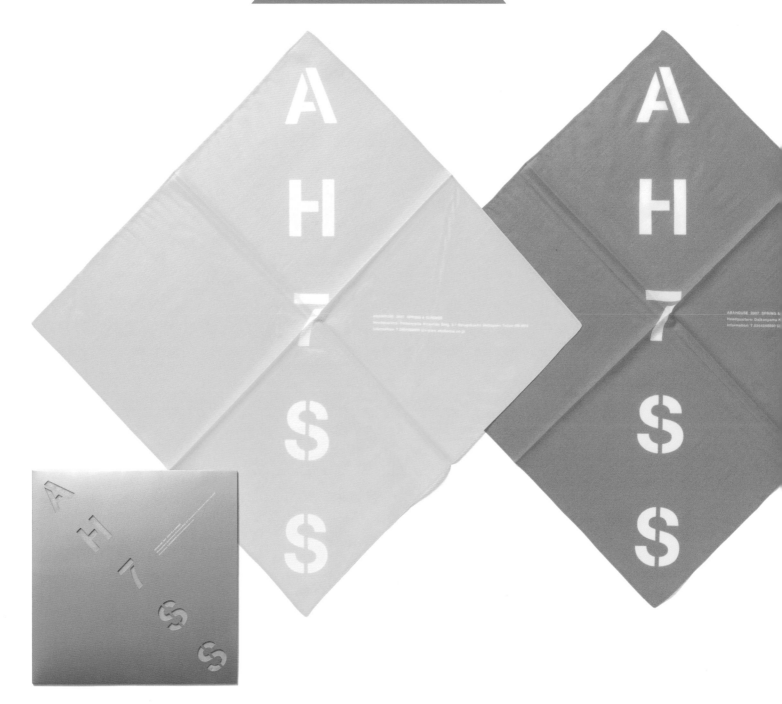

ABAHOUSE
2007年 Spring & Summer
カタログ & ノベルティ

ABAHOUSE：2007 Spring / Summer catalogue and novelty

アパレル Apparel

2007年S/Sのカタログは、ケースの文字が型抜きされ、中から表紙が覗くデザインに。ノベルティのバンダナは春らしい4色で制作し、カタログ同様パッケージの文字が型抜きされ、中の色が見える仕組みとなっている。

The characters on the case of the 2007 Spring / Summer catalogue have been cut out to make the cover of the catalogue visible. The bandana novelty was produced in four spring colors. The characters on the bandana's packaging have been cut out in the same way as the catalogue, so that the different colors can be seen.

配布対象：顧客　狙い・効果：シーズンイメージの伝達
Target market：Customers　Aim and effect：Communication of the season's image

CL：アバハウスインターナショナル　Abahouse International Co.
AD, D：野尻大作　Daisaku Nojiri　P（Person）：北井博也　Hiroya Kitai
P（Clothes）：樋口兼一　Kenichi Higuchi　DF, SB：ground　Japan

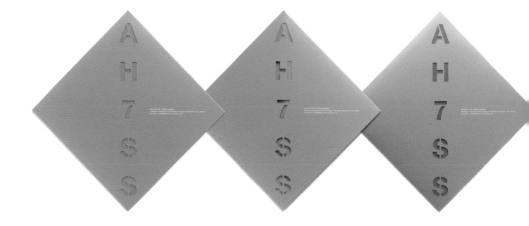

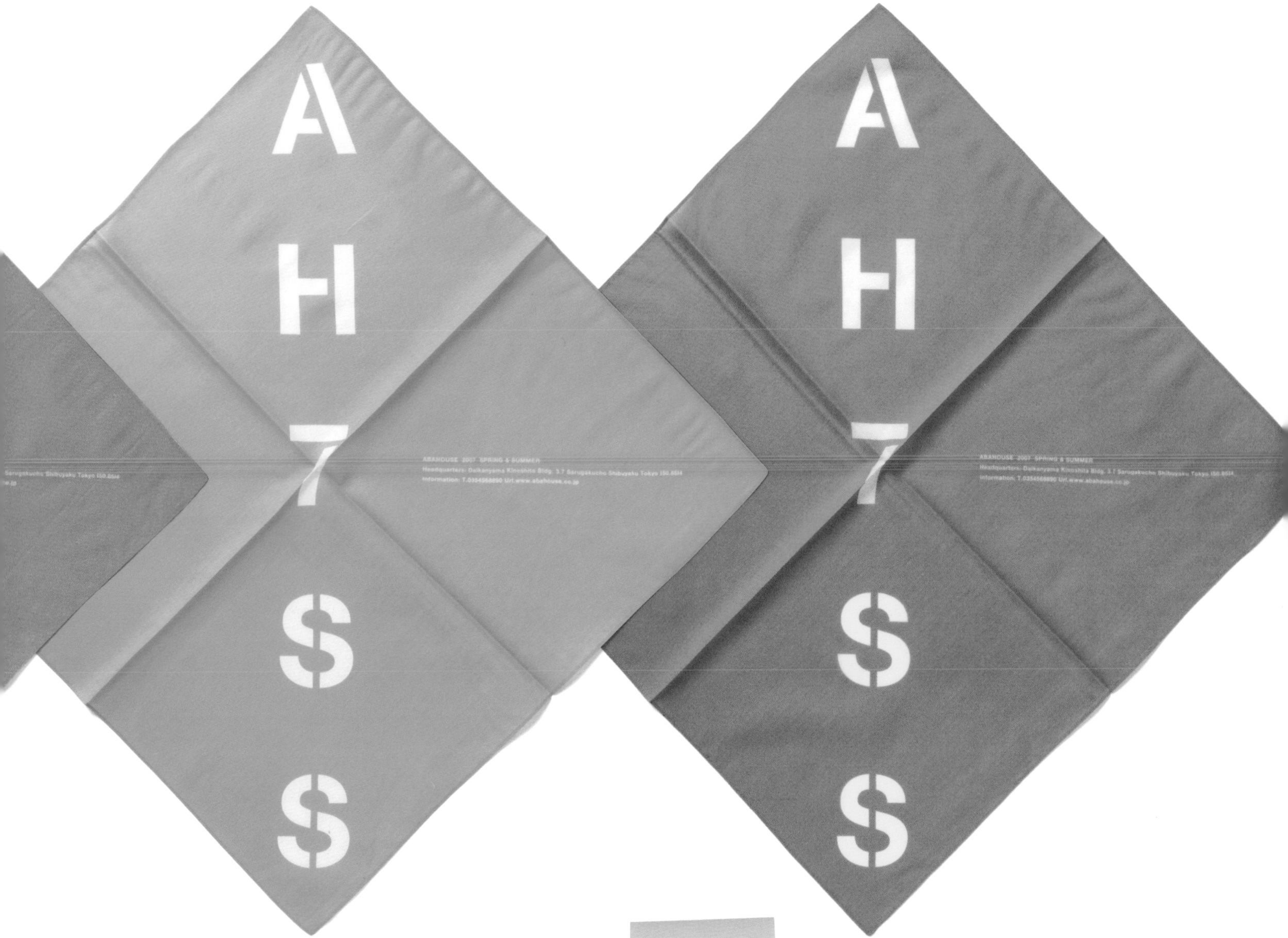
A
H
7
S
S
ABAHOUSE 2007 SPRING & SUMMER

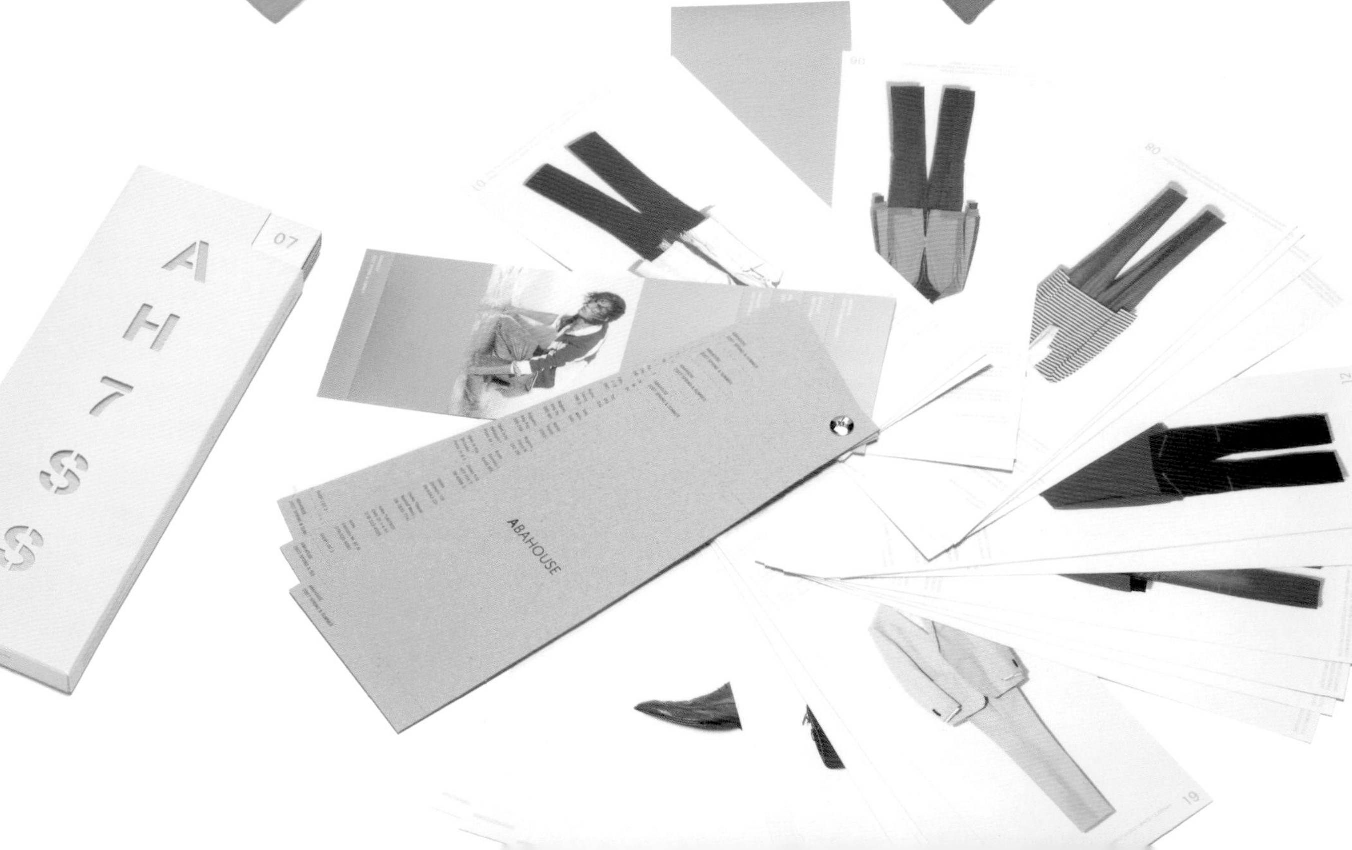
07
A
H
7
S
S
ABAHOUSE

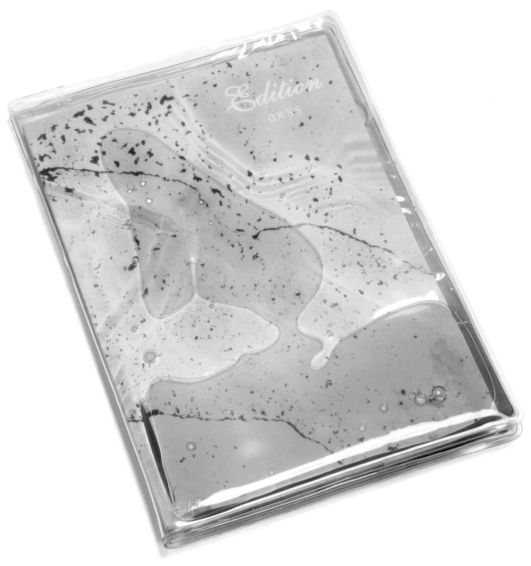

Edition
2008年 Spring & Summer
カタログ

Edition 2008 Spring / Summer Catalogue

アパレル Apparel

ビニールカバーに水色の液体が入ったカタログは、シーズンイメージの「水」をパッケージでダイレクトに表現している。

The catalogue has a plastic cover with blue liquid inside to express the season's image of "water" in the title on the packaging.

配布対象：顧客　配布方法・場所：店頭配布
狙い・効果：シーズンイメージの伝達

Target market : Customers
Distribution method and area : In-store distribution
Aim and effect : Communication of the season's look

CL：トゥモローランド　TOMORROWLAND CO., LTD.
AD：浜田武士　Takeshi Hamada　P：Mitsuo
Agency：INFASパブリケーションズ　INFAS PUBLICATIONS INC.
Artist：TAISUKE KOYAMA　Japan

ラフォーレ原宿「LAFORET PRIVATE PARTY」招待状
LAFORET HARAJUKU : "LAFORET PRIVATE PARTY" invitation

商業施設　Commercial facility

ラフォーレが半年に一度、閉店後に顧客を招いて行なうクローズド・イベントの招待状。招待状としてパーティに持っていくだけでなく、それがあることで会場が盛り上がるものにしようと、メガネ型インビテーションを制作。「プライベートパーティ」のネーミングにちなみ、ちょっといやらしい感じのする目隠しをモチーフに。来場者にはドレスコードとしてその眼鏡型DMをかけてもらい一晩限りの特別なラフォーレを演出した。インビテーションには手の質感を表現するために肌のきめのような質感の紙（アヴィオン）を使用した。

An invitation for a closed event held by LAFORET after store hours every six months with invited customers. The invitation was produced in the shape of eyeglasses, not just as something to bring along to the party, but as a way of livening up the party through the invitation itself. The motif is a somewhat lascivious blindfold to coordinate with the "private party" nature of the event. The guests were required to wear the glasses-shaped DM as part of the dress code. A fine-grained paper (Avignon) was used to impart the texture of a hand to the invitations.

配布対象：顧客　配布方法・場所：郵送　狙い・効果：限定イベントの特別感・限定感を出すことを狙った
Target market : Customers　**Distribution method and area :** Mail
Aim and effect : To express the special and exclusive nature of this event

CL：ラフォーレ原宿 LAFORET HARAJUKU Co., Ltd.　Planning, Produce, SB：電通 DENTSU INC.
Planning, Produce：コモンデザイン室 Common Design Room／アマナ amana inc.　CD, AD：えぐちりか Rika Eguchi
D：古谷 萌 Moe Furuya／湊村歓和 Toshikazu Minatomura／大辻祐介 Yusuke Otsuji／落合剛之 Takayuki Ochiai／
阿部梨絵 Rie Abe　P：田島一成 Kazunari Tajima　P（Event venue）：シトウレイ Rei Shito　Hair make：ABE（H）／Yuki（M）
Retoucher：吉川武志 Takeshi Yoshikawa　CP：和田耕司 Koji Wada　Proof, Printing：日庄 Nissho Corporation　Japan

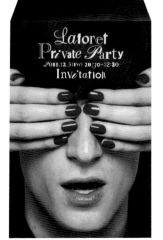

チームマイナス6%×ラフォーレ原宿 コラボイベント「LAFORECO」

"LAFORECO": Team -6% and LAFORET HARAJUKU collaborative event

商業施設 Commercial facility

地球温暖化防止のアクションを考えながら、ショップオリジナルのスタンプでマイバッグをデザインするラフォーレ原宿の参加型イベント「LAFORECO」用に製作されたマイバッグ。参加者が考える地球温暖化防止のアクションを、木の葉をモチーフにした用紙に記入し、木をイメージしたパネルに貼り付けると、マイバッグに各ショップのオリジナルスタンプを自由にレイアウトすることができた。

An eco-bag produced for "LAFORECO", an event run by LAFORET HARAJUKU where eco-bags were designed with original shop stamps as a way of raising awareness of global warming. Participants who wrote down their ideas for ways to prevent global warming on the special form with a motif of leaves and then posted them on the board that resembled a tree were allowed to create their own layout of the original shop stamps on their own eco-bags.

配布対象：イベント参加者　配布方法・場所：ラフォーレ原宿
Target market : Event participants
Distribution method and area : LAFORET HARAJUKU

CL：ラフォーレ原宿　LAFORET HARAJUKU Co., Ltd.
CD, AD：佐野研二郎　Kenjiro Sano
D, I：服部公太郎　Kotaro Hattori　SB：MR_DESIGN　Japan

b6（ビーロク）オープン告知ツール

b6 (B-roku) : Opening announcement

不動産 Real estate

ファッションビル「b6」のオープンに際して配布された街頭配布ノベルティ。明治通りと表参道の大きな交差点近くに位置するロケーションの特徴を活かして制作されたコミュニケーション・マークと、そのマークをテキスタイル柄のように展開させたビジュアルがデザインの軸となっている。「b6」のユーザーとなり得る20代～30代男女をターゲットとしたノベルティは、どれも親しみやすいポップな仕上がりとなっている。

A novelty for street distribution on the occasion of the opening of fashion building b6. The communication mark that utilizes the features of the area around the large intersection between Meiji-dori and Omotesando and visuals that have developed the mark into a textile pattern are the axis of the design. Each of the novelties, targeted at males and females in their 20s and 30s who may frequent b6 have been created in a friendly, pop style.

配布対象： 渋谷から原宿を中心に、b6に買い物に来てくれそうな20～30代を中心とした男女 **配布方法・場所：** b6周辺

Target market : Males and females mainly from the Shibuya to Harajuku areas in their 20s and 30s who may frequent the b6 fashion building **Distribution method and area :** Around the b6 fashion building

CL：エルカクエイ L Kakuei Corp. CD, AD：松下 計 Kei Matsushita
D：田辺智子 Tomoko Tanabe／渡辺京子 Kyoko Watanabe
I：竜田麻衣 Mai Tatsuta／2e／梶野沙羅 Sara Kajino
CW：小島富貴子 Fukiko Kojima Agency：エイム クリエイツ AIM CREATE Co., Ltd.
DF, SB：松下計デザイン室 Kei Matsushita Design Room Inc.
Printing：エイト印刷 Eight Printing Co., Ltd. Japan

Harbour City × Collette ノベルティ

Souvenir umbrellas：
Collaboration between Harbour City × Collette

商業施設 Commercial facility

香港のショッピングモール、ハーバーシティのお土産プレゼントとして制作されたアンブレラ。パリの有名セレクトショップ、コレットのキャラクター「カペリーノ＆ペペローネ」の作者クンゼル＆デガとのコラボレーション。「カペリーノ＆ペペローネ」のパターンをあしらい、赤、黄色、水色の3色で展開。

These souvenir umbrellas with the "Caperino & Peperone" patterns on were produced for Harbour City, a shopping mall in Hong Kong. They were created in collaboration with Kuntzel & Deygas who created the Cap & Pep, the characters of the famous specialty store Collette in Paris. The umbrellas are available in three different colours.

Artwork：Kuntzel & Deygas AD, SB：AllRightsReserved Ltd. Hong Kong

白光堂書店 しおり Hakkodo Shoten Bookmarks

書店 Bookstore

ユーザーとのコミュニケーションを円滑にする目的でデザインされたしおりは、生肉、破れた紙幣、バナナの皮など、どれもユニーク。一瞬本物と見間違うほどにリアルだが、実はどれもイラスト。今まで「しるし」でしかなかったしおりに機能性を持たせることで、本を読むことや、そこから生まれるコミュニケーションをより楽しんで欲しいという願いが込められている。

The raw meat, torn paper money and banana skin bookmarks, each of them unique, were designed for better communication with customers. They look so real that you may be taken in for a second or two, but they are actually just illustrations. The aim of the bookmarks is to increase the enjoyment derived from reading books and communication with customers, by making the humble bookmark, that until now has been used simply to mark a place in a book, into something functional.

配布対象：書籍購入者 配布方法・場所：店頭 狙い・効果：ユーザーとのコミュニケーションがより円滑になった
Target market : Book buyers **Distribution method and area :** Stores
Aim and effect : Better communication with users

CL：白光堂書店 Hakkodo Bookstore AD, D：鎌田順也 Junya Kamada D：宇部信也 Shinya Ube
I：佐藤正樹 Masaki Sato CW：清松俊也 Toshiya Kiyomatsu DF, SB：レバン LEVAN inc. Japan

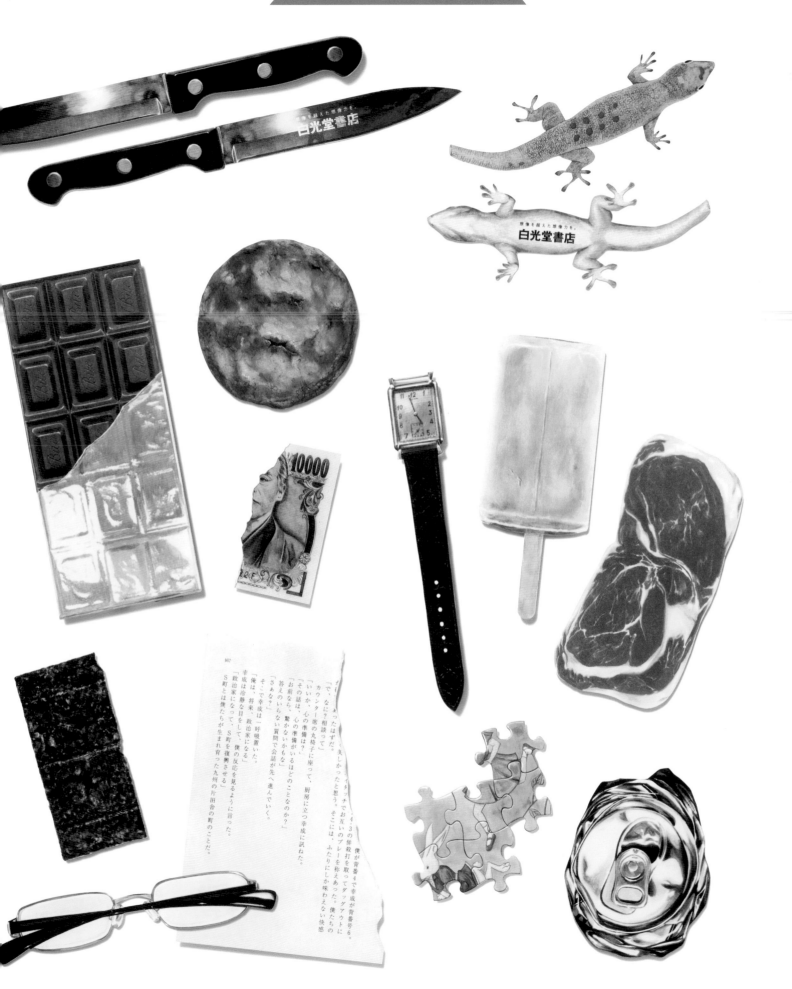

AB-CAFE イベントツール

AB-CAFE : Event tool

カフェ Cafe

オフホワイトの壁に、オフホワイトのデザイナーズチェアでインテリアを統一しているAB-CAFE。店舗の認知向上のために開催されたイベント「TOY-LET」では、本物のトイレをまるでおもちゃのプラモデルトイレのようにデザインした。イベントにあわせて、缶バッジやプラモデルキット、オリジナルパッケージのトイレットペーパーなどが製作された。

AB-CAFE has standardized its interior with off-white walls and off-white designers chairs. At the "Toy-Let" event held to improve recognition of the cafe, a real toilet was designed to look like a toy plastic model toilet. Metal badges, plastic model kits and toilet paper in original packaging were produced for the event.

配布対象：来店者　配布方法・場所：店頭
狙い・効果：カフェの認知向上のため
Target market : Customer of the cafe
Distribution method and area : Cafe
Aim and effect : To improve recognition of the cafe

CL：AB-CAFE　AD, D：小杉幸一　Koichi Kosugi
P：阿部 健　Takeshi Abe
Agency, SB：博報堂　HAKUHODO Inc.　Japan

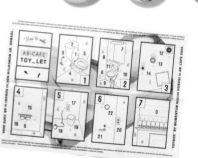

ウツボムーン ショップツール
Utsubo Moon : Shop tools

ライブハウス Club with live music

和歌山県田辺市にあるライブハウスのために作られたマッチ、コースター、コンセプトブック。各ツールにオリジナルフォント（ウツボアヴァンギャルド）を使用しており、カタカナで「ウ」「ツ」「ボ」「ム」「ー」「ン」と一文字ずつ分けてデザインしている。ウツボのイラストもポイントとして使われており、一度見たら忘れない、印象深いデザインとなっている。

Matches, coasters and a concept book produced for a live music club in Tanabe City, Wakayama Prefecture. Original font (utsubo avant-garde) is used for the design and each word is separated in each tools. An illustration of a moray eel (utsubo) has been used a point in each of the shop tools for a design that registers with people and is unforgettable.

配布対象：顧客・来店客 配布方法・場所：店頭
Target market : Customers, visitors to the club
Distribution method and area : Store

CL：ウツボムーン Utsubo moon   AD, D：永井裕明 Hiroaki Nagai
D：高橋かおる Kaoru Takahashi / 藤井 圭 Kei Fujii
P：藤井 保 Tamotsu Fujii   CW：藤原大作 Daisaku Fujiwara
DF, SB：エヌ・ジー N.G. INC.   Japan

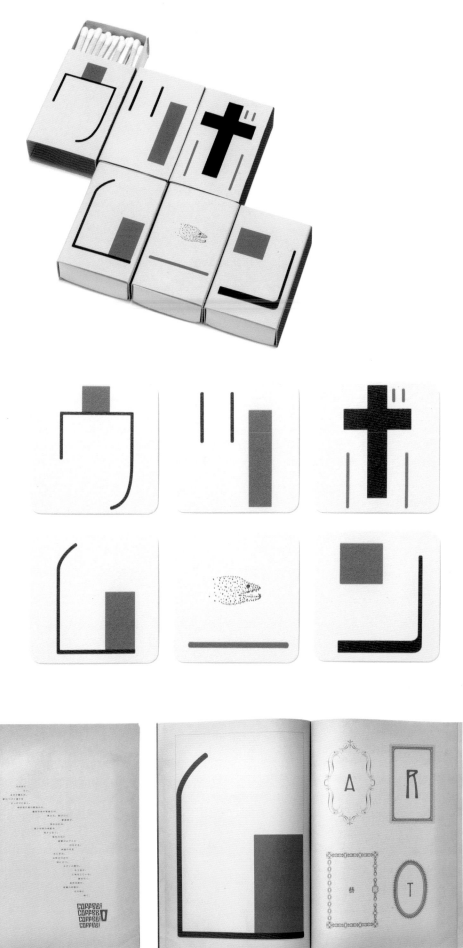

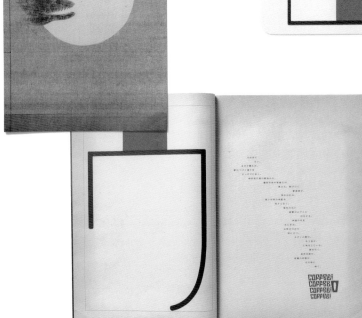

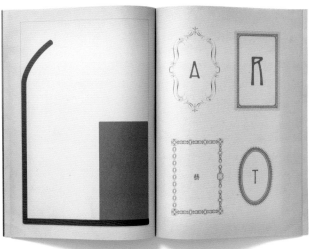

カナリア
オープニングプロモーション

Canaria : Opening promotion

飲食店 Restaurant

同じ空間の中に「カフェ & ダイニング」と「バー & ラウンジ」が存在する飲食店、カナリア。店内の入口は同じだが、用途により案内するエリアが異なる仕組みになっている。「リゾートの昼と夜」という店のコンセプトをもとに白と黒を用い、DMを製作。店舗オープンまでの期待感を高めるため、ロゴのコインのイメージを想起させるカナリアゲーム(オセロゲーム)も同封している。

Canaria, a restaurant where "cafe & dining" and "bar & lounge" coexist within the same space. The restaurant has one entrance but each area within the restaurant is characterized according to its use. Direct mail was produced in the colors of black and white based on the restaurant's concept "Night and Day at the Resort." To increase the sense of anticipation surrounding the opening, also enclosed is the Canaria game (Othello) that resembles the image of the coin on the logo.

配布対象：顧客　配布方法・場所：郵送　制作数：1,000個
狙い・効果：オープニング販促・メンバー獲得。　制作コスト：700,000円
Target market : Customers　**Distribution method and area :** Mail
Number produced : 1,000　**Aim and effect :** Promoting the restaurant's opening, acquisition of members　**Production costs :** ¥700,000

CL：amkユイマール　amk-yuimaru　CD：神 靖幸　Yasuyuki Kon
DF, SB：オペレーションファクトリー　opereation factory
D：エイチツーケーグラフィックス　H2K GRAPHICS　Japan

「GEORGIA × crocs」
コラボレーションキャンペーン
GEORGIA × crocs : Collaborative campaign

飲料 Beverage

缶コーヒー「GEORGIA」を購入すると、crocsのシューズとロゴのチャームがついた、オリジナルストラップがもらえるキャンペーン。全部で6種類あり、ベルト部分にはcrocsのシューズ・アクセサリー「ジビッツ」がつけられる。この他、応募をすると「crocsオリジナルダイアリー」と人気モデル「cayman型USB」が各500名にあたる。どちらも、実用性と面白さを兼ね備えたグッズとなっている。

A campaign where customers receive an original carry-strap with crocs shoes and logo charms when they purchase GEORGIA can coffee. The straps come in six types in all and a Jibbitz shoe accessory has been attached to the strap's belt. In addition, 500 crocs original diaries and 500 of the popular cayman USB will be given out upon request. All the goods are both useful and entertaining.

配布対象：商品購入者・プレゼント応募者　配布方法・場所：店頭
狙い・効果：販売促進
Target market : Purchasers of products, persons who request the campaign gifts　**Distribution method and area :** Stores
Aim and effect : Promoting sales

CL：日本コカ・コーラ　Coca-Cola(Japan)Company, Limited
SB：クロックス エイジア プライベート リミテッド　crocs asia pte. ltd. Japan

※キャンペーンは
終了しています。

オトナグリコ 1

いつだって迎えに来てくれる。

30年…

どうしてくれたのが、家族なんだ。

ワカメ（34）

カツオ（36）

オトナグリコ 3

カツオ、36歳。ひとりで食べるより、

ふたりで食べるほうがおいしい。

と、ボクですら思う。

「ワカメ〜。」

ⓒ長谷川町子美術館

オトナグリコ 4

26歳のイクラ。

28歳のタラオ。

名前のことで文句を言ったり、10代がなつかしい。

ⓒ長谷川町子美術館

ⓒ長谷川町子美術館

オトナグリコ 10

ワカメ、34歳。

私、きちんとした人が苦手だ。

なぜだろう。

ⓒ長谷川町子美術館

アタリ

おめでとうございます！

江崎グリコ「OTONA GLICO」プレゼントキャンペーン

Ezaki Glico : "Otona Glico" gift campaign

菓子製造販売 Confectionary maker

上質な素材を用いた大人向けチョコレート「OTONA GLICO」のキャンペーンのテーマは、「25年後の磯野家」。CMでは、カツオやワカメ、タラちゃん、イクラちゃんといったお馴染みのキャラクターを豪華俳優陣が演じている。キャンペーンマークの付いている「OTONA GLICO」の商品を買うと、4コマ漫画カードがおまけとしてついてくるとともに、アタリが出ると、「25年後の磯野家」スペシャル図書カード（4枚セット）がプレゼントされる。

The theme for the "Otona Glico" campaign featuring chocolate designed for adults produced with high-quality ingredients was "25 years of the Isono family." In the commercial, the familiar characters of Katsuo, Wakame, Tara-chan and Ikura-chan are played by a cast of well-known Japanese actors. If you purchase "Otona Glico" products with a campaign mark, you receive a free yonkoma manga card, and if your card is a winner, you then receive a set of four special "25 years of the Isono family" prepaid cards for purchasing books and magazines.

配布対象：応募者　配布方法・場所：郵送　狙い・効果：販売促進
Target market : People who entered the competition
Distribution method and area : Mail　**Aim and effect :** Promotion of sales

CL：江崎グリコ Ezaki Glico Co., Ltd.　CD：佐々木 宏 Hiroshi Sasaki
AD：水口克夫 Katsuo Mizuguchi　D：山中牧子 Makiko Yamanaka, Odds Design
P：高柳 悟 Satoru Takayanagi　CW：岡本欣也 Kinya Okamoto
Agency, SB：シンガタ Shingata Inc. / 電通関西支社 DENTSU inc. KANSAI　Japan

「25年後の磯野家」スペシャル図書カード（4枚セット）が当たりました。以下の手順で「アタリ」券を応募して下さい。

応募方法　上記の「アタリ」部分を点線から切り取って紙に貼り、（1）郵便番号、（2）ご住所、（3）お名前、（4）電話番号をご記入のうえ、下記宛先に封書でご応募下さい。「アタリ」の半券は、賞品が届くまで、必ずお手元に保管して下さい。（新しい4コマカードも賞品と一緒にお送りします。）
宛先　〒535-8511 オトナグリコ スペシャル図書カード プレゼントキャンペーン（156号）
応募締切　第1回締切2009年1月31日／第2回締切2009年3月31日／第1回締切2009年1月31日／第2回締切2009年5月31日（すべて当日消印有効）※締切後2週間前後で商品を発送致します。
問合せ先　「OTONA GLICO」スペシャル図書カードプレゼントキャンペーン」事務局　06-6955-2438　受付時間：平日9：00〜17：00 土日祝日を除く

※アタリマークの封入がない場合、ご当選は無効となります。※必要事項の記入漏れがあれば、ご当選は無効となります。また、賞品の届け先のご住所・転居先・電話などが不明で連絡が出来ない場合もご当選は無効となります。※当ご当選の権利はご本人のもので、他に譲渡・換金はできません。※個人情報はお客様に断りなしに、業務委託先以外の第三者に開示・提供することはありません。※ご記入いただいたお客様の個人情報は、賞品発送業務のために利用させていただきます。

076

ハーベスト「30周年ありがトート」プレゼントキャンペーン

Harvest "30th anniversary ArigaTote bag": Gift campaign

菓子製造販売 Confectionery sales

発売30周年を記念して実施されたプレゼントキャンペーン。期間中、内袋に「あたり」のシールが貼ってある商品購入者に、もれなくオリジナルトートバッグがプレゼントされた。バッグは、表と裏で色も柄も異なるリバーシブルのデザイン。表はハーベストをモチーフにしたドット柄で華やかに、裏は手書き風のハーベストマークを大きく配してシンプルに仕立てた。パッケージと同じ形にデザインした携帯用ポーチとハーベストマークのキーカバーがセットとなっている。

A gift campaign launched in commemoration of the 30th anniversary. During the campaign period, customers who find a winning sticker inside packets of Harvest confectionary received an original tote bag. The bag has a reversible design in a different color and pattern on each side. One side of the bag is gorgeously decorated with a motif of Harvest bisckets in a dot pattern, and the other, with a simple arrangement of hand-drawn versions of the Harvest mark. A mobile phone pouch designed in the same shape as the packaging and a Harvest mark key cover come as a set.

配布対象：内袋に「あたり」のシールが貼ってある商品購入者　狙い・効果：販売促進
Target market : Customers who find a winning sticker inside packets of Harvest confectionary　**Aim and effect :** Promoting sales

CL, SB：東ハト　Tohato Inc.　Japan

ポテコとなげわ「純銀ポテコ＆純銀なげわ」 プレゼントキャンペーン

Poteco and Nagewa
"Pure silver Poteco and pure gold Nagewa": Gift campaign

菓子製造販売 Confectionery sales

お菓子自体がリングの形をしており、指にはめて食べる楽しさが魅力である商品ということから、それに合ったプレゼントを考案。リング形状をデザインした「純銀ポテコ」や「純銀なげわ」、「ポテコ」と「なげわ」のキャラクターが時計の針になった「オリジナル目覚まし時計」があたるキャンペーンを企画した。商品の魅力を広めるとともに、家族揃って楽しめるものを目指した。

The gift was devised around the idea of ring-shaped snack that is fun to put on your finger and then eat. A campaign was planned where you could win "pure silver Poteco" and "pure silver Nagewa" rings and an original alarm clock with Poteco and Nagewa characters as the hands on the clock. The aim was to create a gift that not only increased the popularity of Poteco and Nagewa products, but was fun for the whole family.

配布対象：商品購入者　狙い・効果：販売促進
Target market : Customers of Poteco and Nagewa products
Aim and effect : Promoting sales

CL, SB：東ハト　Tohato Inc.　Japan

住商フルーツ「甘熟王」プレゼントキャンペーン

Sumifru : "Kanjukuo" gift campaign

フルーツ輸入・販売 Fruit import and sale

住商フルーツが販売するバナナ「甘熟王」のプレゼントキャンペーン用景品と宣伝素材。「老若男女問わず幅広い人たちに親しまれ、長く愛されること」をコンセプトにデザインされたバナナの王様「甘熟王」をキャラクターとし、純金製の同キャラクターを抽選でプレゼントするキャンペーンを展開した。

The gift and the advertising material for the "Kanjukuo" gift campaign for bananas sold by Sumifru. The Kanjukuo banana king character was designed with the concept in mind of "being embraced and highly regarded by a large number of people of all ages over a long period of time." Part of the campaign was a lottery, the prize being a version made from gold of the banana king character.

配布対象：プレゼントキャンペーン応募者　制作数：1個（金の甘熟王）、866個（銀の甘熟王）、450個（バナナセラー）、3,000個（バナナケース）　狙い・効果：ブランドの認知向上

Target market : People requesting the campaign gifts　**Number produced :** 1 (Gold Kanjukuo), 866 (Silver Kanjukuo), 450 (Banana cellar), 3,000 (Banana case)　**Aim and effect :** Improving brand recognition

CL：住商フルーツ SUMIFRU CORPORATION　CD：岩井博文 Hirofumi Iwai　AD：横川信之 Nobuyuki Yokokawa
CW：成田真樹 Maki Narita　Agency：ADKインターナショナル ADK International Inc. / ADK ASATSU-DK INC.
DF, SB：ドリームデザイン dreamdesign co., ltd.　Japan

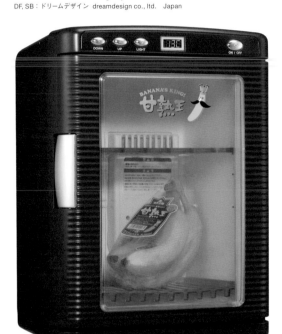

ポスター Poster

ネスカフェ
「これでもかコレクション」
プレゼントキャンペーン

Nescafé : "How about this one?" collection -
Gift campaign

食品・飲料　Food and Beverage

50人のデザイナーがデザインしたエコバッグとマグカップのプレゼントキャンペーン。同じかたちのバッグとマグカップを使うことと「ハッピーなコーヒー気分＆コーヒータイムを表現する」という共通したテーマ以外は、全てデザイナーたちの自由な感性に任せられている。

A gift campaign featuring eco-bags and mugs designed by 50 different people. Each of the designers was left to come up with his or her own design for exactly the same bag and mug with the theme of "happy coffee feeling & coffee time."

配布対象：ネスカフェ対象商品購入者へ向けたクローズド懸賞　制作数：100,000個　狙い・効果：新規ユーザーの獲得。初年度のジョイントプロモーションにも関わらず高い認知率を獲得し、30代以下を中心に多くの応募があった

Target market : Closed prize contest towards purchasers of certain Nescafé products

Number produced : 100,000

Aim and effect : Acquisition of new users. Achieved a high level of recognition despite not doing much joint promotion in its first year, and received a large number of submissions, mainly from the under-30s.

CL, SB：ネスレ日本　Nestlé Japan Ltd.
CD：奥田 淳　Jun Okuda
AD：山室実花子　Mikako Yamamuro /
新里 碧　Midori Niisato　P：藤井春日　Haruhi Fujii /
坪谷靖史　Yasushi Tsuboya
CW：葛谷晴子　Haruko Kuzuya
Agency：マッキャンエリクソン　McCann Erickson Japan Inc.
Japan

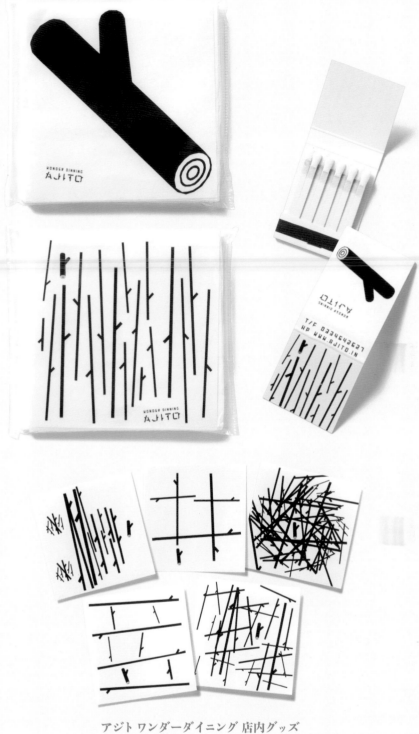

アジト ワンダーダイニング 店内グッズ

Ajito Wonder Dining : In-store goods

ダイニングバー Dining bar

渋谷の一角にある隠れ家ダイニングバー、アジトは、子どもの頃の秘密基地をイメージした雰囲気づくりを目指している。「何か」を作り出す元となる一つのピースとして、昔、秘密基地を作るときに使用した「枝」をモチーフとして、ティッシュペーパー、マッチなど様々な媒体に展開した。

A dining bar tucked away in a corner of Shibuya, Ajito's aim is to create an atmosphere that brings back memories of the hiding places we had as children. Various goods including tissue paper and matches were developed on various media, with a motif of the branches used to create those hiding places from long ago.

配布対象：来店者　**配布方法・場所：**店頭　**狙い・効果：**店内の統一感・イメージの定着
Target market : Customers of the dinig bar　**Distribution method and area :** Dining bar
Aim and effect : Achieve a sense of consistency throughout the restaurant, establish the bar's image

CL：アジト ワンダーダイニング AJITO WONDER DINNING　AD, D：小杉幸一 Koichi Kosugi
Agency, SB：博報堂 HAKUHODO Inc.　Japan

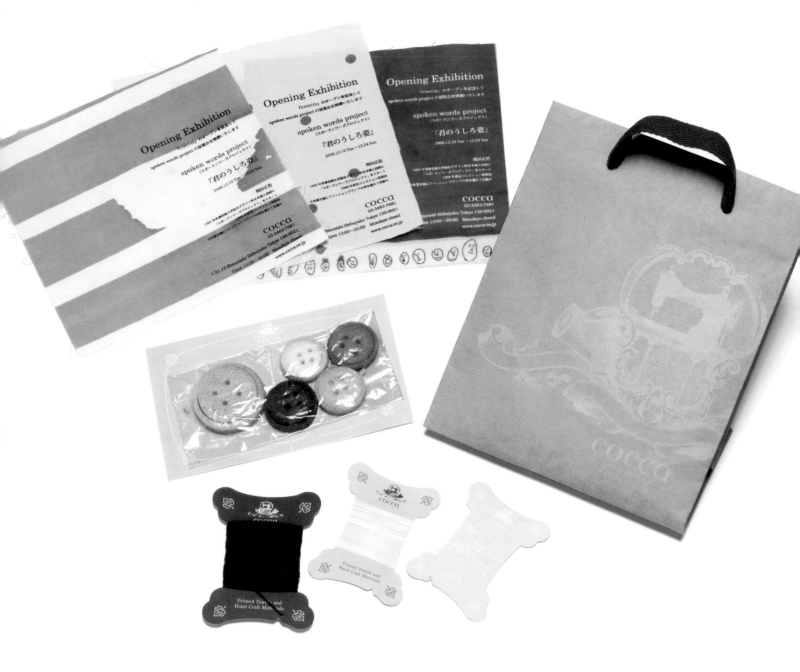

cocca オープニングノベルティ

cocca : Opening novelty

ファブリックブランド　Fabric brand

衣食住全般のライフスタイルを提案するファブリックブランド cocca。インビテーションは、オリジナルファブリックに印刷して制作し、ボタン型のクッキーやオリジナルのポケットティッシュケースは、オープニング来場者にプレゼントした。糸巻き型のショップカードに本物の糸を巻き付けて同封するなど、手づくりにこだわるブランドの姿勢が感じられるノベルティとなった。

Fabric brand cocca that offers a lifestyle of food, fashion and home décor. The invitation was printed onto original fabric and button-shaped cookies and original pocket tissue cases were presented to guests at the launch party. Novelties such as the spool-shaped shop cards around which real thread had been wound sent a strong message about a brand that highly values the art of the hand-made.

配布対象：顧客・来店者　配布方法・場所：店頭で手渡し
Target market : Customers, visitors to stores
Distribution method and area : Hand delivery at stores

CL, SB：cocca　　CD：バーデンバーデン　BadenBaden
AD, D (Invitation)：KLOKA GRAPHICS
D (Pocket Tissue Cover)：spoken words project　Japan

もくきんど キャンペーンノベルティ
mokukindo campaign novelty

器専門店　Specialty tableware

上質でこだわりのある器を販売する、もくきんどのオリジナルラ
ンチョンマット。並べるとグラスを持った手の影たちが乾杯してい
るように見える仕組みとなっている。手づくりの食器を販売する
店ならではの心温まる表現を目指した。キャンペーン期間であった
夏をイメージして、メッシュになっている刺繍用の布を使っている。

An original luncheon mat from mokukindo, a store selling high-quality tableware. The mat is designed with a set of silhouettes of hands
holding glasses, raised for the making of a toast. The aim was the
kind of heartwarming expression only found in a shop that sells
hand-made tableware. An image of summer, the season in which
the campaign was run, and mesh embroidery fabric were used.

配布対象：対象商品購入者　配布方法・場所：店頭配布
制作数：200枚×4パターン
Target market : Purchasers of certain mokukindo products
Distribution method and area : In-store distribution
Number produced : 200 × 4 patterns

CL：もくきんど　mokukindo　AD, D：内田雅之　Masayuki Uchida
P：堺 浩二　Koji Sakai　CW：原 晋　Susumu Hara
Agency, SB：東急エージェンシー　Tokyu Agency Inc.　Japan

アークガーデン 10周年記念ノベルティ
Ark Garden：Tenth anniversary commemorative novelty

総合ディベロッパー　Urban developer

アークヒルズにあるサントリーホール屋上庭園「ルーフガーデン」（非
公開）の特別一般公開の告知ポスター用に撮影された写真を使用
し、アークガーデン10周年記念のノベルティグッズとして製作され
た布製のエコバッグ（撮影・ホンマタカシ氏）。アークガーデンの魅
力が伝わる美しいデザインに仕上がっている。

A cloth bag (photo by Takashi Homma) produced as the Ark
Garden tenth anniversary commemorative novelty, with the
same photograph used on posters announcing the special
opening to the general public of the Suntory Hall Roof Garden
in Ark Hills, usually closed to the public. The bag has a beautiful design that conveys the charm of Ark Garden.

配布対象：アークガーデン利用客他
Target market : Users of Ark Garden etc.

CL, SB：森ビル　Mori Building Co., Ltd.
P：ホンマタカシ　Takashi Homma　Japan

フェザー「髭（HiGE）× FEATHER」コラボキャンペーン

FEATHER : "HiGE × FEATHER" collaborative campaign

剃刀の製造・販売 Production and sale of razors

ロックバンド「髭（HiGE）」とフェザー安全剃刀のコラボレーションキャンペーン。バンドのキャラクター「ハイジ」を使用したオリジナルの商品を展開した。また、フェザーのCMソング「髭よさらば」をカップリングしたシングルCD「夢でさよなら」をタワーレコード各店で購入すると貰えるステッカーも制作した。

A collaborative campaign between the rock band HiGE (also the Japanese word for facial hair) and the FEATHER Safety Razor Company. Original products were developed using the band's character of Heidi. Stickers were produced for customers at Tower Records stores who bought the CD single "Farewell in a Dream" that was coupled with the song that featured in the FEATHER commercial "Farewell to facial hair."

配布対象：髭（HiGE）のニュー・シングル購入者　配布方法・場所：タワーレコード各店で先着プレゼント
Target market : Customers of HiGE's new single
Distribution method and area : Gift for the first purchasers of CD at Tower Records stores

CL：フェザー安全剃刀 FEATHER　CD, AD, CW：堀内弘誓 Hirochika Horiuchi　AD：福森正紀 Masaki Fukumori
D：脇田紘之 Hiroshi Wakita / 郷原永資 Yosuke Gohara　CW：芦田裕美子 Yumiko Ashida
Agency：電通 関西支社 DENTSU INC. KANSAI　DF, SB：スリーアンドコー Three & Co.　Japan

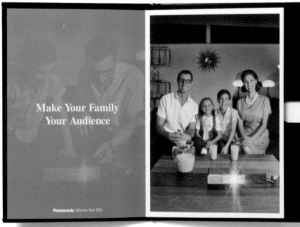

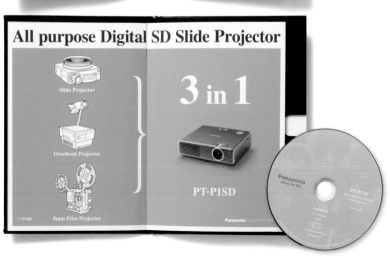

パナソニック「PT-P1SD」プレスキット

Panasonic "PT-P1SD" : Press kit

電気機器の生産・販売 Production and sale of electrical appliances

かばんに入れて持ち運ぶこともできる、軽量型液晶プロジェクターの海外用プレスキット。プロジェクターで映し出された映像を楽しむ家族をキービジュアルとしている。

The overseas press kit for the lightweight LCD projector that can be carried around in a bag. The key visual is a family enjoying the images they are viewing with the projector.

配布対象：プレス関係者　制作数：約1,000個
Target market : Media-related persons　**Number produced :** approx. 1000

CL：パナソニック Panasonic Corporation　AD, D：石浦 克 Masaru Ishiura
DF, SB：TGB design.　Japan

「OFFICE LIFE NEWS」
登録キャンペーン
"Office Life News": Registration campaign

総合ディベロッパー Urban developer

六本木ヒルズ、アークヒルズなど森ビルが管理・運営するオフィスで
働くオフィスワーカーに向けて配信される、メールマガジン「OFFICE
LIFE NEWS」配信規模の拡大に伴う登録キャンペーン。様々な場所
に貼ってもらい、普段から会員であるという意識を高めてもらえる
ように入会者にはステッカーを配布。オフィスワーカーを対象としたフッ
トサル大会も開催され、賞品としてTシャツと王冠も製作した。

A registration campaign for Office Life News, an e-mail magazine delivered to office workers in Mori Buildings at Roppongi
Hills, Ark Hills etc, as a means of increasing its readership. Stickers were distributed to new members so that they could stick
them in various places and let other people know that they were
members. T-shirts and other products were manufactured for
the winners of the futsal tournaments held between members.

配布対象：森ビルが管理・運営するオフィスで働くオフィスワーカー
配布方法・場所：入会者にはステッカーを封入し郵送した **狙い・効果：**より多く
のオフィスワーカーに、会員となる意味や楽しさを伝えるため、インパクトのある
マークと展開方法を考案。結果、メールマガジンの認知度アップにつながった
Target market : Office worker working in Mori Buildings
Distribution method and area : Stickers were enclosed in envelopes
and posted to new members. **Aim and effect :** To communicate to a
greater number of office workers the meaning and the fun of becoming an
Office Life News reader, a high-impact mark and a way of developing the
campaign were devised. There was, as a result, increased recognition of
the e-mail magazine.

CL：森ビル MORI BUILDING CO., LTD.
AD：藤本やすし Yasushi Fujimoto D：瀧 加奈子 Kanako Taki
DF, SB：キャップ CAP CO., LTD. Printing：レーエ re-e CO., LTD.
Japan

「the SOHO -TOKYO BAY NEW YORK STYLE-」
オリジナル ミニ ジェンガ
"the SOHO-TOKYO BAY NEW YORK STYLE" : Original mini-JENGA

不動産 Real estate

「the SOHO」は、東京臨海副都心の青海に世界最大級のSOHOビルディングを建設するプ
ロジェクト。24時間「働く」「遊ぶ」「クリエイトする」をテーマとしたこのプロジェクトのプ
レス発表会のお土産として、高さ20cmほどのカラフルなミニジェンガが配られた。

"the SOHO" is a project to build the world's highest-grade SOHO building in the sea-
side sub-metropolis of Aomi in Tokyo. As a souvenir of the press conference held to
announce the project that is based on the themes of "work, play and create 24 hours
a day," colorful mini-JENGA sets of approximately 20cm in height were distributed.

配布対象：マスコミ関係者 **配布方法・場所：**プレス発表会場
Target market : Media-related persons
Distribution method and area : Press conference held to announce the project

CL：プロパスト PROPERST CO., LTD. AD, D, SB：グルーヴィジョンズ groovisions Japan

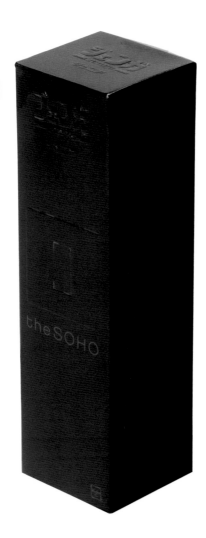

今、僕が、一番言いたかったことは、つまり、もしもあなたに言えるとしたら何ていうだろう。ありがとう、ごめ

彼女と出会った時、「よりやく好きな人ができそうでことを覚えたのに。それを感じさせ成績で言えば、「愛職人」の彼女は僕はどんどん嘉分同じ大学を出ていたこともよく大学

３年が続った七夕の夜、僕らは別れることになった。メンの味なんて、もう一生味わうことはないと思う。結ばれた日を選ぶっていうじゃないか、って思ったけことを〈くだらないな〉っていうだけど良くは買うことができ別れたことを意識した。

彼女を初めて一緒にした大きな買い物の、このオーディオだった。将来、もし、一緒になったら──そうさせようにも言わなかったけど、らジカセで音楽を聴くことれる右上々ないでいどうせ買うなら、将来一緒になっても、使い続けピアノのようないつやの黒い大きくても小さくもないところがスピーカーの首感も言ってから流れ

だけど前のように思えとにかく、ほんの少し前のことがも思える。僕が東京に来て、一番最初にしたことは、とにかくもうサントリーの真ん中に据ったのは、田舎から運ばれてたりロックバンドが好だった僕の頭のっ右方でその延びていた。曲も中に聴々き込んだ、「ロックバンドが好だ田舎から運んで来たカセットのコードがたかった。見上げる天井のぼんやりとその近くに済んでいなかった。蛍光灯を付けるソケットがあって、彼になる前に明かりをつけなきゃな、と、ぼんやり考えていた。

ソニー「System501」店頭配布用ブランドブック
Sony "System501": Brand book for store distribution

電気機器のマーケティング・セールス
Marketing and sale of electric machinery

「本棚サイズの本格オーディオ」から生まれた、文庫本サイズのブランドブック。短編小説と写真で、商品の世界観を描いた。カバーにトレーシングペーパーを使用することで、文庫本にはつきものの帯とカバーを両立。表紙の柄がうっすらと透き通って見えるデザインは、音楽に浸る幻想的なひとときをイメージしている。

A brand book in pocket edition size created from the idea of "a real audio system in bookshelf size." In a short story format with photographs, the book describes the philosophy of this product. A balance between the cover and the obi, or strip of paper that is wrapped around pocket editions, is achieved by using tracing paper for the cover. The faintly transparent pattern on the cover creates an image of a magical time indulging oneself in one's favorite music.

配布対象：第1弾 団塊世代・第2弾 30～40代女性
配布方法・場所：第1弾 大手量販店他System501コーナー・第2弾 ソニーショールーム「ソニービル」System501コーナーにて設置、配布
狙い・効果：音楽が持ち歩くものになった今の時代に、部屋で音楽を聴くことの良さを、ストーリーと写真を通して再発見してもらいたい

Target market : Volume 1 baby boomers, then females in their 30s and 40s
Distribution method and area : Volume 1 the System501 section of major merchandise stores etc, then distributed at the System501 section of the Sony showroom in the Sony Building **Aim and effect :** In a world where music has become something that people listen to on the move, through stories and photographs, to rediscover the greatness of listening to music in the comfort of one's own home.

CL：ソニーマーケティング Sony Marketing (Japan) Inc.
CD：原田 朋 Tomoki Harada AD, D：中谷佳保里 Kahori Nakatani
P (#1-1)：渋谷健太郎 Kentaro Shibuya P (#1-2)：松井聡美 Satomi Matsui
P (#1-3)：百々 新 Arata Dodo P (#2-1)：橋本昌幸 Masayuki Hashimoto
P (#2-2)：杉田知洋江 Chiyoe Sugita
Naming & CW & Story (#1-1)：小櫟 元 Gen Kogusuri
Story (#1-2)：中村 航 Kou Nakamura Story (#1-3)：黒澤 光 Hikaru Kurosawa
Story (#2-1)：村山由佳 Yuka Murayama Story (#2-2)：市川拓司 Takuji Ichikawa
Stylist：百々奈津美 Natsumi Dodo Agency, SB：博報堂 HAKUHODO Inc.
Printing：三浦印刷 MIURA PRINTING CORPORATION Japan

ロート製薬「AOHAL CLINIC」開院記念グッズ

Rohto Pharmaceutical Co. Ltd. "AOHAL CLINIC"
Anniversary commemorative goods

美容皮膚クリニック Skin-care clinic

ロート製薬によってスタートした「Well Aging（より良く年齢を重ね、より充実した人生を送るという考え方）」をテーマとする「AOHAL PROJECT」の一環としてオープンした、スキンケアに関するサービスや情報を提供するクリニックの開院記念ノベルティ。「美しい肌」に貢献できるグッズとしてタオル、ピルケースを選択し、品質にもこだわったタオルはクリニックのマークを生かしたパッケージングを施している。

A range of novelty goods commemorating the opening of the clinic that provide information about the clinic's skin-care services, as a part of the AOHAL Project featuring the theme of "Well Aging" (an approach to dealing with the aging process better and to living one's best life) launched by Rhoto Pharmaceutical. The goods including towels and pill cases were chosen for their contribution to beautiful skin, and were wrapped up in the high-quality towel that bears the clinic's symbol.

配布対象：患者　配布方法・場所：クリニック
Target market : Patients　**Distribution method and area :** Clinic

CL：ロート製薬 ROHTO Pharmaceutical Co., Ltd.　CD, AD：居山浩二 Koji Iyama
D：赤土桂子 Yoshiko Akado　DF, SB：イヤマデザイン Iyamadesign　Japan

小山動物病院 オリジナルグッズ　KOYAMA ANIMAL HOSPITAL : Original goods

医療 Medical care

動物病院であるため、猫をキャラクター化し、ステッカーやTシャツなどのグッズにおとしこんだ。来院客に親しみを感じてもらえるよう、DMや薬袋も同キャラクターを使用したデザインとなっている。

Because it is an animal hospital, a cat character was created and stickers and T-shirts were produced based on that shape. To impart a sense of friendliness to visitors to the hospital, direct mail and medicine bags were designed using the same cat character.

配布対象：来院客　**Target market :** Visitors to the hospital

CL：小山動物病院 KOYAMA ANIMAL HOSPITAL　CD, CW：西尾ヒロユキ Hiroyuki Nishio
AD, D, I：池澤 樹 Tatsuki Ikezawa　Agency, SB：東急エージェンシー Tokyu Agency Inc.　Japan

Salon オープンノベルティ
Salon Opening novelty

ヘアサロン　Beauty salon

国内外の第一線で活躍しているトップスタイリストが集結してオープンしたヘアサロン「Salon」のノベルティ各種。アートディレクションを担当した水野氏が「高級ホテルのような演出を目指した」というプレスキットやメイキング写真集（コンセプトブック）、トートバッグなどのグッズは、金箔押し加工によってゴージャスさを表現している。

Various novelties produced for the new hair salon, Salon, featuring top stylists who have worked in Japan and overseas. The gorgeousness of the goods that include a press kit, a "the making of" photographic collection (concept book) and a tote bag for which Mizuno who was in charge of art direction wanted "the production design of a high-quality hotel" was expressed with a gold foiling process.

配布対象：プレス関係者
Target market : Media-related people

CL：Salon　AD：水野 学　Manabu Mizuno
D：相澤千晶　Chiaki Aizawa　PR：小野由紀子　Yukiko Ono
DF, SB：グッドデザインカンパニー　good design company
Japan

Sheep 顧客用ノベルティ Sheep : novelty for customers

ヘアサロン Beauty salon

自分がもしも違う髪型だったらどんな風に見えるかを試せるように、手鏡の鏡の部分に髪型がついているグッズを制作。あくまで、おもちゃとして楽しんでもらうため少し変わった髪型も混ぜている。また、顧客にこんな髪型どうですか？と提案できるように、ダイレクトメールとしても送付できる仕組みとなっている。

A novelty hand mirror produced with different hairstyles on the mirror part itself so that people could see how they would look in them. Slightly bizarre styles were also included as the novelty was designed as a plaything. The mirror was sent to customers in the form of a direct madil together with the suggestion "How about this hairstyle?"

配布対象：美容院利用客　配布方法・場所：店頭配布・ダイレクトメール　制作数：600個
Target market : Salon customers　**Distribution method and area** : Distribution in salon, mail.　**Number produced** : 600

CL：シープ　Sheep　AD, D：内田雅之　Masayuki Uchida　I：ricco.
Agency, SB：東急エージェンシー　Tokyu Agency Inc.　Japan

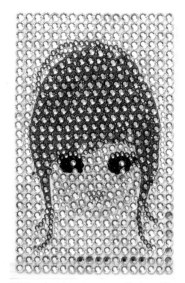

携帯デコレーションシール Decorative mobile phone stickers

コンパクトミラー
Compact mirror

「Hot Pepper Beauty」オープン記念キャンペーン
"Hot Pepper Beauty": Commemorative campaign

クーポン・マガジン Coupon magazine

ヘアサロン検索サイトのオープンを記念してプレゼントされた、世界でたった3つの限定リカちゃん人形。髪型をはじめ、身につけている服や靴までがオリジナルでデザインされた。携帯版検索サイトのオープン時には、スワロフスキーストーンでリカちゃんがデザインされた携帯デコレーションシールとコンパクトミラーをプレゼントした。

Three limited edition Rika dolls, the only ones of their kind in the world, presented in commemoration of the launch of the hair salon search website. Not only Rika's hairstyle but the clothes and shoes she is wearing are original designs. When the mobile search site was launched, the campaign gift was decorative mobile phone stickers and a compact mirror with Rika designed in Swarovski crystals.

配布対象：プレゼント応募者　**Target market :** People who requested the campaign gift

CL：リクルート RECRUIT CO.,LTD　CD：山崎隆明 Takaaki Yamazaki／松本恭彦 Yasuhiko Matsumoto
AD：永江達史 Tatsushi Nagae　D：村井亮介 Ryosuke Murai／小林るみ子 Rumiko Kobayashi
CW：松本恭彦 Yasuhiko Matsumoto／石田 潤 Jun Ishida　DF, SB：クリエーティブ・パワー・ユニット CREATIVE POWER UNIT
AGENCY：電通関西支社　DENTSU INC. KANSAI　Japan

「ポイコ」プロモーションツール
Poico : Marketing tool

ポイントカード Points card

対象の飲食店（ポイコ加盟店）に行くとポイントがたまり、たまったポイントで割引やプレゼントのサービスを受けることができる「ポイコ」。「P」のロゴと水色＆ピンクの配色をキービジュアルとし、店頭のプロモーションツールにおとし込んだ。加盟店では箱入りガムを配布、店員は缶バッジを身につけることで、ポイコの認知度アップにつながった。

The Poico card with which you can receive discounts and other free offers using the points you have accumulated by frequenting the participating restaurants (Poico members). The letter P of the logo and the blue and pink were key visuals and used in the marketing tools for the restaurants. Poico's level of recognition was increased by distributing boxes of gum at participating outlets and staff members wearing Poico metal badges.

対象：来店者・加盟店
Target : Restaurant customers, participating restaurants

CL, SB：リクルート　RECRUIT CO., LTD.
CD, CW：児島令子　Reiko Kojima
CD, AD, D：服部一成　Kazunari Hattori
D：山下ともこ　Tomoko Yamashita　Japan

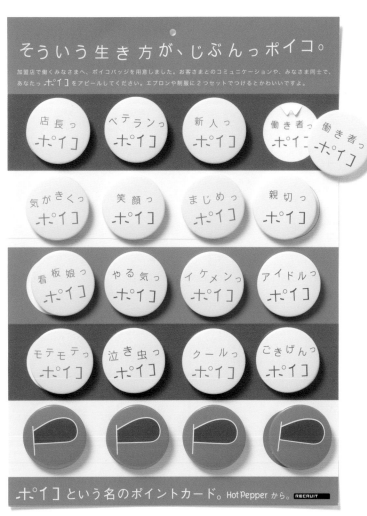

テイクアンドギヴ・ニーズ販促ツール
TAKE and GIVE NEEDS : Marketing tools

結婚式場 Wedding venue

結婚式場、テイクアンドギヴ・ニーズ来館者にパンフレットを入れて渡される
サプライズバッグ。最初は平らな状態で接客時に会話をしながら組み立ててバッ
グにするため、来館者に驚きと喜びを与えることができる。サプライズをモットー
にしているテイクアンドギヴ・ニーズのファーストサプライズ。

A surprise bag containing brochures that are handed out to wedding guests
at the TAKE and GIVE NEEDS wedding venue. The bags are presented to
guests in flat form at the beginning and as it progresses, the guests as-
semble the bag as they converse with each other, an idea that surprise and
delights everyone present.

配布対象：来館者　配布方法・場所：全国のテイクアンドギヴ・ニーズ会場
狙い・効果：ウェディングパンフレットを入れる袋としては画期的な試みだったため、会場
の認知度向上につながった
Target market : Wedding guests　**Distribution method and area :** TAKE and GIVE
NEEDS wedding venues throughout Japan　**Aim and effect :** It increased the
recognition of the wedding venue because it was a revolutionary idea for the bag for
the wedding pamphlet.

CL：テイクアンドギヴ・ニーズ　TAKE and GIVE NEEDS Co., Ltd.
CD, CW：武藤雄一　Yuichi Muto　AD, D：安田由美子　Yumiko Yasuda
DF, SB：アイルクリエイティブ　ayr creative　Japan

ネットドリーマーズ
創業9周年記念ノベルティグッズ
9th anniversary of founding of Net Dreamers : Novelty goods

IT事業 IT business

関係者・クライアント・社員に創業9周年の感謝の意を伝えるための記念ノベルティグッズ。ビジネスシーンで使えるものをテーマに、リングノートやメモ帳が製作された。9周年にちなんで9個のアメも配られ、実用性とともにユーモアのあるノベルティを目指した。

Commemorative novelty goods for the expression of appreciation to clients, employees and other related people on the occasion of the 9th anniversary of the founding of the company. As the novelty was to be something that would be usable in a business environment, a spiral-bound notebook and memo pad were produced. Nine candies for every year since the founding were distributed also, the aim being a novelty that is humorous as well as useful.

配布対象：関係者・クライアント・社員 配布方法・場所：社内 制作数：180（ダブルリングノート・メモパッド）・166（キャンディ） 狙い・効果：9周年の社員への感謝を込めて製作・社員の団結へとつながった 制作コスト：280,000円 / 単価：1,556円（ダブルリングノート）・275,500 / 単価：1,530円（メモパッド）・55,000円 / 単価：331円（キャンディ）
Target market : Related-persons, Client, Staff **Distribution method and area :** In the office **Number produced :** 180 (Note, Memo pad), 166 (Candy) **Aim and effect :** Produced as a token of appreciation to employees who have been with the company for nine years, leading to solidarity with employees. **Production costs :** ¥280,000 / unit price : ¥1,556 (Double ring note)・¥275,500 / unit : ¥1,530 (Memo pad)・¥55,000 / unit : ¥331 (Candy)

CL：ネットドリーマーズ Net Dreamers AD：美澤 修 Osamu Misawa D：竹内 衛 Mamoru Takeuchi I：斎藤 茜 Akane Saito SB：omdr Co., Ltd. Japan

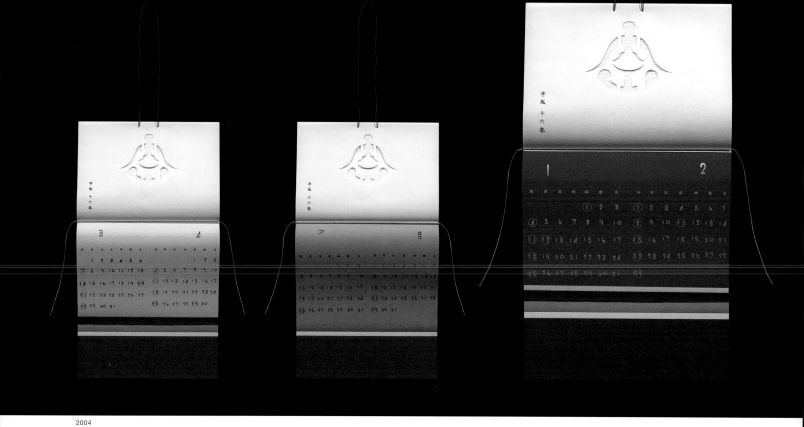

2004

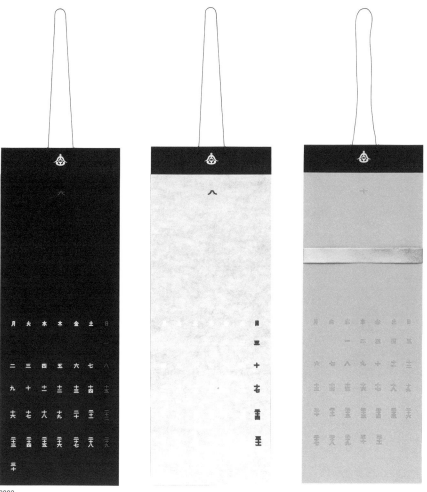

2003

播磨社寺工務店カレンダー
Harimashaji Koumuten calendar

工務店 Builder

宮大工の播磨社寺工務店のルーツは鎌倉時代まで遡り、600年余り受け継がれてきた在来工法で、社寺建築の修繕・改築を行っている。神社や寺に配るため、社寺建築の空間にマッチするようにデザインされている。

Harimashaji Koumuten, a carpentry firm specializing in the constructions of shrines and temples, originated in the Kamakura era, and repairs and reconstructs shrine and temple buildings with traditional methods of construction that have been passed down over 600 years. As it is distributed to shrines and temples, the calendar has been designed to complement the architectural spaces of these places.

配布対象：神社・寺 配布方法・場所：手渡し・郵送 制作数：50個
制作コスト：1,000,000円
Target market : Shinto shrine, Buddhist temples
Distribution method and area : Hand delivery, Mail
Number produced : 50 **Production costs :** ¥1,000,000

CL：播磨社寺工務店 Harimashaji Koumuten Co., Ltd.
AD, D：北川一成 Issay Kitagawa
DF, Printing, SB：グラフ GRAPH   Japan

KDDI「au one」プロモーションツール
Promotion tools for KDDI "au one"

通信 Communications

KDDIが2007年9月に開始した、携帯電話向けポータル「EZweb」と、PC向けポータル「DION」などを統一したポータルサイト「au one」のノベルティグッズ。マグカップ、ルービックキューブ、携帯ストラップなど、同ポータルサイトのオリジナルキャラクター「auワン」をデザインしたグッズが多数製作されている。

Novelty goods for the "au one" portal site created from the merging of the EZweb mobile phone portal launched by KDDI September 2007 and the DION PC portal, among others. A large range of goods including mugs, Rubic cubes and mobile carry-straps was produced using the portal site's original character.

配布対象：KDDI利用者　**配布方法・場所**：郵送
Target market：User of KDDI
Distribution method and area：Mail

CL：KDDI KDDI Corporation　CD, AD：佐野研二郎 Kenjiro Sano
D：榮 良太 Ryota Sakae　SB：MR_DESIGN　Japan

ジェットスター 日本初就航搭乗者記念ノベルティ

Jetstar : Japan-Australia inaugural flight commemorative novelty

航空輸送業 Aviation transportation industry

日本就航第一便搭乗者へプレゼントされた、ジェットスタービーチセット（ビーチバッグ・ビーチボール・ビーチタオル）。3月は、日本はまだ寒い季節だが、オーストラリアは夏。現地の海やビーチで楽しく過ごしてもらうために、ビーチセットを用意した。

A Jetstar beach set (beach bag, beach ball and beach towel) presented to passengers on the inaugural flight between Japan and Australia. Although it is still cold March in Japan, in Australia it is late summer. The beach set was created for passengers to enjoy themselves on the beaches of Australia.

配布対象：ジェットスター日本就航第一便搭乗者　配布方法・場所：関西国際空港　制作数：1,200個
狙い・効果：ブランドロゴの認知度向上　制作コスト：3,650円
Target market : Passengers on the inaugural flight between Japan and Australia
Distribution method and area : Kansai Airport　**Number produced :** 1,200
Aim and effect : Recognition of the brand logo increased.　**Production costs :** ¥3,650

CL：ジェットスター Jetstar Airways　Agency：オグルヴィ PR Ogilvy PR　Processing：Make Merry
SB：オグルヴィ・パブリック・リレーションズ・ワールドワイド・ジャパン Ogilvy Public Relations Worldwide (Japan), Tokyo Japan

西濃運輸 会社説明会 販促ツール

Seino Transportation : Recruiting tools

物流 Distribution

缶コーヒーを飲む機会の多い業界にちなみ、オリジナル缶コーヒーを制作。缶の側面には、「東大生も助手席から」「乙女の誕生日に安全靴をくれる人がいます」など、西濃運輸ならではのコピーが入った吹き出しシールが貼られ、人事担当者と学生とを繋ぐ大切なコミュニケーションツールとして活用されている。缶は青と黄色を基調とした配色で、本物の缶コーヒーに西濃運輸らしさが上手くブレンドされている。

An original can coffee was produced for its association with an industry where a lot of can coffee is consumed. On the side of the can are speech bubble stickers containing typically Seino Transportation-type messages which serve as an important communication tool for connecting the human resources managers and students.

配布対象：就職活動の学生　配布方法・場所：就職活動イベントブース・就職説明会　制作数：1,800
狙い・効果：吹き出しのシールが学生とのコミュニケーションにつながった
Target market : Student job-seekers　**Distribution method and area :** Booths at recruitment events, employment seminars　**Number produced :** 1,800　**Aim and effect :** The speech bubble stickers establish communication with the students.

CL：西濃運輸 Seino Transportation Co., Ltd.　CD：竹中圭一 Keiichi Takenaka　AD, D, I：平井秀和
Hidekazu Hirai　CW：加納広明 Hiroaki Kanou　Agency：リクルートメディアコミュニケーションズ Recruit Media Communications　DF, SB：ピースグラフィックス Peace Graphics　Japan

空堀ことば塾 プロモーションツール
Promotional Tool for Karahori-Kotoba Private School

学習塾 Private school

ルドルフ・シュタイナーが創始したヴァルドルフ教育を実践する寺子屋、空堀ことば塾。詩や物語を中心に、独自のカリキュラムで小学生が思考し、表現する能力をじっくりと育てることを目指している。のびのびと学習できるよう、子どもが使用する各ツールは風合いのある、ナチュラルな素材で制作。ポスターや作文用紙のデザインに使用されている色も、昔の赤青鉛筆のような素朴なイメージとした。

Karahori-Kotoba Juku, a private school offering supplementary lessons outside school hours that practices the Waldorf method of education founded by Rudolf Steiner. The aim of the school's unique curriculum consisting mainly of poetry and literature is to make school children think for themselves and to nurture their ability for self-expression. Each of the tools used by the children is produced in highly textured natural materials. The colors used in the design of the posters and the writing paper has a simple image that resembles the red and blue pencils of olden days.

配布対象：子ども（生徒）・親　**配布方法・場所：**教室
Target market : Children (students) and parents
Distribution method and area : Classroom

CL：空堀ことば塾　Karahori-Kotoba Private School
AD：八木義博　Yoshihiro Yagi　D：木村 洋　Yo Kimura
I：市田千絵　Chie Ichida　CW：筒井晴子　Haruko Tsutsui
Agency, SB：電通関西支社　DENTSU INC. KANSAI
DF：カタチ　Katachi Co., Ltd.　Printing：アートファクトリー　art factory
Silk screen：滋賀芸術学舎　Shiga Art School　Japan

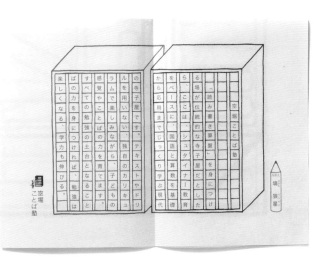

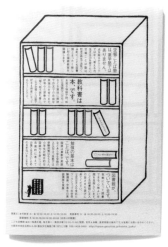

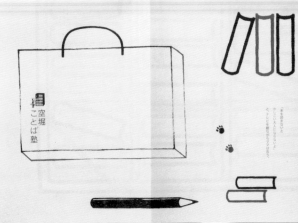

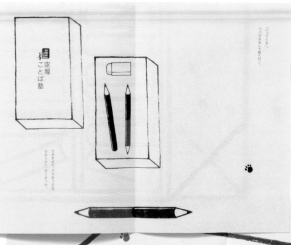

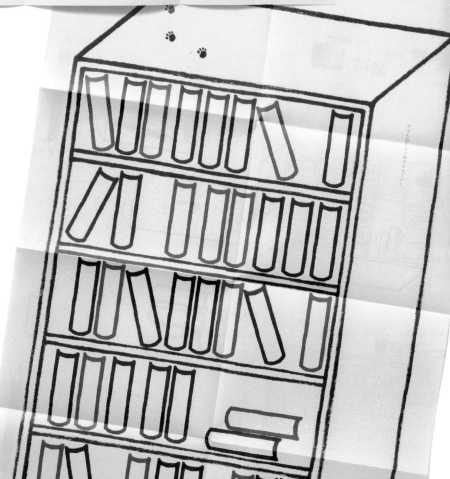

ポスター　Poster

「広告小学校」教材 & ノベルティ

"Advertising Primary School"
teaching materials and novelty

教育 Education

CMづくりを通して思考力・判断力・表現力を養う小学生のためのメディア・リテラシープログラム、「広告小学校」。オリジナルキャラクターとして「コマ犬」を制作し、各ツールのキービジュアルとしておとし込んだ。参加する小学生には、教材として「発見ノート」「解決ノート」「表現ノート」が渡され、オリジナルの定規や下敷きをプレゼントするなど、楽しくプログラムに参加してもらうためのツールが制作された。

A media literacy program, Advertising Primary School, for primary schoolchildren to develop their intellect, judgment and expression through the making of commercials. An original character was produced and used as a key visual in each of the tools. Primary school children who participated were given a Discovery Book, a Solutions Book and an Expression Book to use on the course, as well as an original ruler and pencil board, a set of tools designed to enhance the fun of the program.

配布対象：プログラム参加者
Target market : Program participants

CL：東京学芸大学附属世田谷小学校　Setagaya Elementary School
AD, D, I：田中 元　Gen Tanaka　SB：電通　DENTSU INC.
Japan

下敷き Pencil board

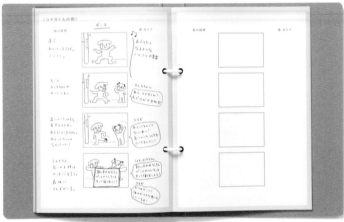

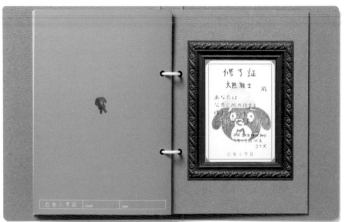

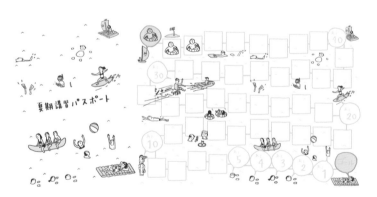

明光義塾 夏期講習限定ノベルティ

Meikogijuku : Summer course limited novelty　　**学習塾 Private school**

明光義塾に来れば、楽しく勉強できるということを子どもたちに伝えるため、ロゴマークのリニューアルに合わせて動物キャラクターを制作。また、広告物やリーフレットにもCMと連動したイラストを使用し、親しみやすいデザインとした。ペットボトルホルダーやタンブラーは、夏期講習に参加し、スタンプがたまるともらえる仕組みになっている。

To convey the idea to children that the Meikogijuku was a fun study environment, an animal character was produced to coincide with the redesign of the juku's logo. Illustrations that linked to the television commercials were used in the advertising and leaflets also to create a friendly design. PET bottle holders and tumblers were given out for participation in the summer course and accumulating a certain number of stamps.

配布対象：夏期講習参加者　**Target market :** Summer course participants

CL：明光ネットワークジャパン　MEIKO NETWORK JAPAN CO., LTD.　CD：黒須美彦　Yoshihiko Kurosu
AD：水口克夫　Katsuo Mizuguchi　D：田中貴浩　Takahiro Tanaka　Agency, SB：シンガタ　Shingata Inc.　Japan

牛乳消費拡大キャンペーン
Milk consumption expansion campaign

農業組合　Agricultural association

九州生乳販連が行なった「牛乳消費拡大キャンペーン」の一環として、Webページへの誘引と消費の拡大を目的に製作したノベルティ。牛乳パックの形をしたストラップとレシピ付Web紹介用ハガキをセットにし、2連貼のB倍ポスター上に取り付けて九州各県の鉄道駅構内や街頭に掲出された。

A novelty produced to encourage people to visit the association's website and to increase the number of milk consumers, as part of the milk consumption expansion campaign launched by the Kyushuseinyuhanren. A novelty set consisting of a carry-strap in the shape of a pack of milk and a recipe card encouraging people to visit the website are placed on posters displayed at railway stations and on streets throughout Kyushu.

配布対象：九州エリアの消費者全般
配布方法・場所：街頭サンプリング・駅貼り特殊ポスター・九州各県
狙い・効果：WEBのアクセス数増加と牛乳の消費拡大につながった
Target market : Consumers throughout Kyushu
Distribution method and area : Street sampling, special posters displayed at stations, all Kyushu prefectures　**Aim and effect :** The campaign led to an increased number of visitors to the website and an increase in milk consumption.

CL：九州生乳販連　Kyushuseinyuhanren　CD：植原政信　Masanobu Uehara
AD：常軒理恵子　Rieko Tsunenoki　D：松元孝博　Takahiro Matsumoto
I：漫画コーディネイト／YS　Manga Coordinate / YS
Novelty Planning：山本謙一郎　Kenichiro Yamamoto／夏井英樹　Hideki Natsui
Agency, SB：電通九州　DENTSU KYUSHU INC.　DF：アド・パスカル　AD-PASCAL
Japan

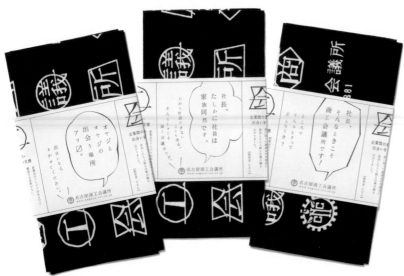

商工会議所 てぬぐい　Chamber of Commerce hand towel

商工会議所　Chamber of Commerce

商工会議所は、お役所的・カタイ・おじさんの集まり・自分には関係ない、そう考えている経営者に興味をもってもらうためのツールを作ることを心がけた。商→そろばんの珠、工→歯車、会→名刺と名刺を合わせる、議→テーブル、所→建物・末広がりで安心感のある形、のイメージでデザイン。帯は、コピーを替えて4種類作成し、親しみやすさと商売上手な老舗感（真面目さ）を感じてもらえることを目指した。

There are many managers who believe the Chamber of Commerce (shokokaigisho) to be a bureaucratic, fuddy-duddy bunch of middle-aged men, and that has no bearing on their lives. The idea, therefore, was to create a tool that would capture the interest of these managers. The wrap-around paper strip comes in four types with interchangeable copy, and the aim was to make recipients aware of a friendly yet serious institution that has been around for many years and is very good at doing business.

配布対象：中小企業の経営者・個人事業主　配布方法・場所：ビジネス系のイベント　制作数：3,000個
狙い・効果：若い経営者や女性経営者など、今まで商工会議所に縁のなかった人とのコミュニケーションにも役立っている

Target market : Managers, trades people in small to medium-sized businesses
Distribution method and area : Business events　**Number produced :** 3,000
Aim and effect : Useful for establishing communication with the people who had not had much to do with the Chamber of Commerce, including young managers and female managers

CL：名古屋商工会議所　NAGOYA CHAMBER OF COMMERCE & INDUSTRY
AD, D, CW：平井秀和　Hidekazu Hirai　DF, SB：ピースグラフィックス　Peace Graphics
てぬぐい制作：たつみ屋　Tatsumiya　Japan

商工会議所 しおり

Chamber of Commerce : Bookmark

商工会議所　Chamber of Commerce

絶版となっていた名古屋ビジネス歴史小説の再発版に挟み込まれたしおり。この小説にしおりを挟むことで、商工会議所への入会促進を目的としている。色とコピーを効果的に使ったデザインで、しおりという限られたスペースが存分に活かされている。しおりは全16種類。擦れて本が汚れないよう、ニス引き加工が施されている。

A bookmark used for the reprinted version of an historical novel about the Nagoya business world that has been out of print. The bookmark was inserted into the novel to encourage new members to the Chamber of Commerce. The design that makes effective use of color and copy maximizes the limited space on the bookmark. The bookmark comes in 16 types and bookmarks have been varnished to prevent the book from getting dirty from the rubbing of the bookmark.

配布対象：書籍購入者　配布方法・場所：本に差し込み・書店カウンター
制作数：9,000個　狙い・効果：名古屋経済界に関わってきた名古屋商工会議所をしおりを用いることで印象的に感じてもらい、入会促進を狙った

Target market : Book purchasers
Distribution method and area : Inserted into books, available at bookstore counters　**Number produced :** 9,000　**Aim and effect :** An image was presented using a bookmark of the Nagoya Chamber of Commerce, a member of the Nagoya economic community, the aim being to promote new membership.

CL：名古屋商工会議所　NAGOYA CHAMBER OF COMMERCE & INDUSTRY
AD, D, CW：平井秀和　Hidekazu Hirai
DF, SB：ピースグラフィックス　Peace Graphics
Printing：コスモクリエイティブ　Cosmo Creative　Japan

バンタンデザイン研究所
2009年度 入学案内パンフレットキット
Vantan Design Institute : 2009 enrollment guide brochure kit

クリエイター養成学校 Creative professions training institute

スクールカラーである赤の外装を開封すると、英語で学校名や学科名がプリントされたトートバッグが現れ、その中に入学案内などが入っている。クリエイティブ思考の強い入学希望者が多いことを意識して、バンタンのオリジナルファッションアイテムとして制作された。入学案内もレイアウトにこだわり、モデルを起用するなどファッションカタログに近い仕上がりとなっている。

A tote bag imprinted with the school and course name in English can be seen when you open the outer packaging that is in the institute's traditional red, and inside the tote bag are the enrollment guides. Realizing there would be strong interest in enrolling in the institute from highly creative people, the brochure kit was produced as an original Vantan fashion item. The layout of the enrollment guide is meticulous and has achieved a fashion catalogue look with the use of models etc.

配布対象：入学検討者　配布方法・場所：ホームページからの資料請求者へ送付
制作数：30,000 個　狙い・効果：クリエイティブ思考の強い対象者向けに、バンタンのオリジナルファッションアイテムとして制作
Target market : People considering enrolling in the institute
Distribution method and area : Sent to people who request information from the website
Number produced : 30,000　Aim and effect : Produced as an original Vantan fashion item for highly creative people.

CL：バンタンデザイン研究所 VANTAN DESIGN INSTITUTE
AD：高橋伸幸 Nobuyuki Takahashi　D：堀場佳代子 Kayoko Horiba /
鏑木佐和 Sawa Kaburaki
DF, SB：スリーミン・グラフィック・アソシエイツ 3MIN. GRAPHIC ASSOCIATES
Printing：アルファ Alpha　Japan

LA CASA ENCENDIDA プロモーションツール

Promotion tool for LA CASA ENCENDIDA

文化施設 Cultural Institution

スケジュール帳とアドレス帳の2分冊で構成されたリサイクル可能な手帳。「0（ゼロ）」の部分がベルクロテープになっており、2冊の接着・取り外しができる。毎年アドレスを書き写さずに済み、環境にも優しい。プロモーションツールとして、会議やイベントの際に配られた。

Recycle agenda divided in 2 sections, address book and agenda. Then stick together through a velcro that goes all around the zeros. You do not need to write down all your contacts again every year.

配布方法・場所：会議・イベント　制作数：2,000　制作コスト：35,000ユーロ（約430万円）
Distribution method and area : Events, Meeting　Number produced : 2,000　Production costs : €35,000

CL：LA CASA ENCENDIDA　DF, SB：BASE DESIGN S.L　Printing：Orient　Spain

「Schwarzer Peter der Globalisierung」プロモーションツール
Promotion tool for "Schwarzer Peter der Globalisierung"

行政 Public administration

欧州サッカーリーグを例に、政治・経済、グローバル化などを説明するというユニークな切り口の展覧会のプロモーションツール。同展は、UEFAチャンピオンシップの開催地であるドイツ9都市を巡回した。社会格差、文化的固有性など6グループに分けられたカードには、各トピックの説明とユニフォームをアレンジした衣装を着たモデルが載っており、ババ抜きの要領で遊べる。

This is a card game developed for the exhibition "Fanshop of globalization". Economic mechanism, political backgrounds and cultural context of the economic changes worldwide are discussed by describing corresponding examples of Football.

配布方法・場所：開催地のファッションゾーン 他　**制作数**：1,000個（無料で配布）・2,000個（販売用）　**制作コスト**：4,000ユーロ（約48万円）
Distribution method and area：Fan zones etc.　**Number produced**：1,000 (for free)・2,000 (for sale)　**Production costs**：€4,000

CL, Organization & Texts：The Federal Agency for Civic Education（BPB）　Idea & Concept：raumtaktik / Friedrich von Borries /
Matthias Böttger / Martin Germann / Peter Kasza / Tobias Kurtz / Katharina Rohde　Organization & Texts：Raul Gersson / Arne Busse
AD, D, SB：onlab　AD, D：Nicolas Bourquin / Cathy Larqué / Maria Tackmann / Thibaud Tissot　Fashion Designer：bel epok + Salon
Hugmeyer / Florinda Schnitzel ＋tricotar：substratdesign：urban speed：vonWedel & Tiedeken　P：Piet Truhlar
Styling：Mark Meisser für Basics　Hair & Make-up：Soraya Aurad für Basics　Photostudio：rent-one.de　Models：Valeta Behrens /
Dora Kawyoz / Stefan Riedner / Christin Speich / Hendrik Woitkowiak　Font：TSTAR von binnenland / Mika Mischler
Printing：Keuledruck Ulla Blix & Thomas Götz GbR　Germany

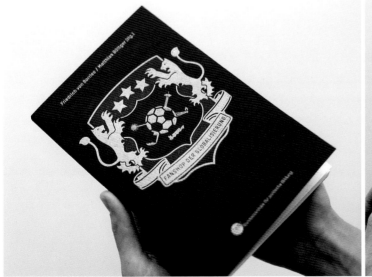

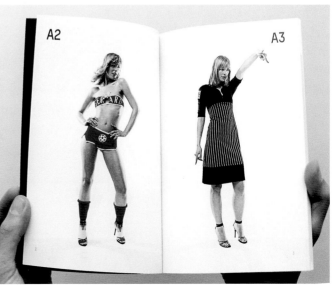

INVITATION

Opening Party for Press
Date : October 3 (Fri)
Time : 3 p.m. to 6 p.m.
Place : NTT InterCommunication Center (ICC)

HOW TO COOK DOCOMODAKE?
Docomodake Art Exhibition in ICC
Date : October 4 (Sat) - 13 (Mon) *closed : 6 (Mon)
Time : 10 a.m. to 6 p.m.
Place : NTT InterCommunication Center (ICC)
http://www.ntticc.or.jp/

Admission : Free
Sponsor :
Team "Docomodake Addict"
http://docomodake.net/art/

INVITATION

「HOW TO COOK DOCOMODAKE ?」
プレスキット&フライヤー
"How To Cook Docomodake ?": Press kit and flyer

展覧会 Exhibition

NTTドコモの広告キャラクターとして誕生した「ドコモダケ」をアート、ファッション、イラストレーション、食など、さまざまなジャンルで次世代を担うアーティストが"料理する"展覧会の巡回展。プレスキットは、ピザのパッケージの中にインビテーションを同封し、郵送した。フライヤーも「食」にからめ、チョコレートバーと割り箸&ナプキンをモチーフに制作。中身は会場でご堪能下さいというコンセプトで、思わず手に取りたくなるフライヤーに仕上げた。

A touring exhibition where next-generation artists of various genres including art, fashion, illustration and food "cook" the Docomodake character produced for Docomo advertising. The invitation was mailed out in a pizza box. The food concept was incorporated into the flyers also and they were produced with a motif of chocolate bars, disposable chopsticks and napkins, making it impossible not to take one.

配布対象：マスコミ関係者・学生etc　配布方法・場所：郵送・学校内
狙い・効果：来場促進
Target market : Media-related persons, students etc.
Distribution method and area : Mail, at schools
Aim and effect : Increase exhibition traffic

CL：NTT DoCoMo　Planning, Produce, SB：電通 DENTSU INC.
Planning, Produce：コモンデザイン室 Common Design Room
CD, AD, Planning, Art work：えぐちりか Rika Eguchi
D：湊村敏和 Toshikazu Minatomura／大上裕未 Yumi Ohue
CW：細川美和子 Miwako Hosokawa　PR：樋口令子 Reiko Higuchi
Planning：山田 遊 Yu Yamada／幅 允孝 Yoshitaka Haba
P：青山たかかず Takakazu Aoyama　CG：吉川武志 Takeshi Yoshikawa
AE：岡本有吾 Yugo Okamoto／吉野谷綾子 Yoshinoya Ayako
Proof, Printing：日庄 Nissho Corporation　Japan

オープニング パーティでの料理　Dishes for the opening party

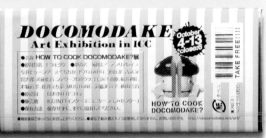

LET'S TASTE DOCOMODAKE!

みなさまご存知ドコモダケは、ドコモの広告から生まれたキャラクター。
その魅力を世界に広めるべく、昨年10月NYにて、ドコモダケを自由に料理してもらうイベントが開かれました。
腕をふるったのは、ペインティングやイラストレーション、写真、彫刻、ファッションなど、
さまざまなジャンルで活躍する日本の次世代アーティスト。
大好評を博したその味わいにリクエストが相次ぎ、日本でも開催する運びとなりました。
ICCという会場ならではのニューテイストも加わっています。
甘いものからビターなものまで、思い思いに味つけされたドコモダケ。あなたもぜひ、ひとかじりしてみてください。

HOW TO COOK DOCOMODAKE?
Docomodake Art Exhibition in ICC

Date : October 4(Sat)-13(Mon) ＊close:6(Mon)
Time : 10 a.m. to 6 p.m.
Place : NTT InterCommunication Center [ICC]

新宿区西新宿2-2-2 東京オペラシティタワー4F
http://www.ntticc.or.jp/

Admission : Free Sponsor : Team "Docomodake Addict" Official HP : http://docomodake.net/art/

ポスター Poster

山口県立美術館
「ピカソ展 幻のジャクリーヌ・コレクション」
オリジナル文庫本

Yamaguchi Prefectural Art Museum
" Picasso – the metamorphosis of the form"

美術館 Art Museum

本展の「愛」というテーマをしっかり伝えるためのツールとして文庫本を作成。ポスターやチラシでは伝えきれない二人の出会いから結婚までの物語が、事実に基づいたフィクションで描かれている。書店以外でも文庫本と認識されるよう、紙質から書体、文字組みに至るまで、本来の文庫本以上にリアルな作りになっている。

A paperback book was produced as a tool to convey the theme of the exhibition, that of love. The story of how two people meet and get married that is not necessarily conducive to portrayal on posters and in brochures was recorded in paperback form in a "fiction based on fact" style. For the paperback to be recognized as such although outside the realms of a bookshop, the book was designed to be even more realistic than real paperbacks, from the quality of the paper, the typeface and the typesetting.

配布対象：山口県および近郊の人 **配布方法・場所**：美術館周辺のお店・美術館内
狙い・効果：展覧会に際しての予備知識としてはもちろんのこと、展覧会後に読めば、より一層満足感や充実感を得ることができる
Target market : People from throughout Yamaguchi Prefecture and environs
Distribution method and area : At the Museum and at shops in the vicinity of the Museum
Aim and effect : By reading the story, firstly as background reading before seeing the exhibition and then after the exhibition also, visitors were able to obtain an even greater feeling of satisfaction and sense of fulfillment.

CL, CD：山口県立美術館 Yamaguchi Prefectural Art Museum
AD, D：野村勝久 Katsuhisa Nomura　I：岡本よしろう Yoshiro Okamoto
CW：大賀郁子 Ikuko Oga　Web Designer：平山智也 Tomoya Hirayama
DF, SB：野村デザイン制作室 NOMURA DESIGN FACTORY
Printing：大村印刷 Omura Printing Co., Ltd.　Japan

島根県立石見美術館
「モダンガールズあらわる。昭和初期の美人画展」
あぶらとりシート

IWAMI ART MUSEUM
"Modern Girls, Blossoming Beauties of the Early Showa Era"

美術館 Art Museum

昭和初期のおしゃれなモダンガールズのイメージとピッタリな「あぶらとりシート」をノベルティに採用。鑑賞後も展覧会の一部を気軽にポーチに入れて持ち歩けるという実用性も兼ねている。またレトロでポップかつビビッドなロゴデザインは、「モダンで洗練された」イメージをアピールしている。

The novelty chosen for the exhibition was oil-absorbing sheets, a perfect fit for the chic image of the Modern Girls of the early Showa period. The sheets have a practical application also. Even after it is over, you can carry a part of the exhibition around with you in a handy pouch. The retro design with its pop and vivid elements has a modern and sophisticated appeal.

配布対象：展覧会の来館者(先着順) **配布方法・場所**：美術館 **狙い・効果**：展覧会の雰囲気に合わせたノベルティにすることで、来館者に鑑賞するだけではない楽しみを提供した
Target market : Visitors to the exhibition (first come, first served)
Distribution method and area : Art Museum
Aim and effect : By selecting a novelty that suited the style of the exhibition, visitors were given enjoyment in addition to the exhibition itself.

CL：島根県立石見美術館 IWAMI ART MUSEUM　AD, D：野村勝久 Katsuhisa Nomura
DF, SB：野村デザイン制作室 NOMURA DESIGN FACTORY　Printing：大村印刷
Omura Printing Co., Ltd.　Japan

山口県立美術館「モディリアーニと妻ジャンヌの物語展」
告知用しおり&マップ

Yamaguchi Prefectural Art Museum
" Modigliani and Hébuterne, The tragic couple "

美術館　Art Museum

モディリアーニへの認知を高めるべく、本に挟めるクイズ形式のしおりを作成。本の表紙のような文様枠を入れることで、展覧会のコンセプトである「物語性」を印象付けた。しおりの紐の色にも青と赤と白を使って、統一感を出している。

A bookmark in quiz format was produced to raise the public's recognition of Modigliani. The use of a patterned frame that resembled the cover of a book brought out the concept of the exhibition, that of telling a story. Blue, white and red were also used for the string on the bookmark to achieve a sense of consistency throughout.

配布対象：山口県および近郊の人　配布方法・場所：小中学校・美術館内・美術館周辺のお店
狙い・効果：気軽にとってもらえるために、しおりのサイズに。クイズの種類が多いので、集める楽しさから展覧会の集客につながることを狙った

Target market : People from throughout Yamaguchi Prefecture and environs
Distribution method and area : Primary and middle schools, at the Museum and at stores in the vicinity of the Museum　Aim and effect : A bookmark, easy to hand out, was chosen for its size. As there was a large selection of quizzes, the aim was connecting the visitors to the exhibition through the pleasure of collecting them.

CL：山口県立美術館　Yamaguchi Prefectural Art Museum　AD, D：野村勝久　Katsuhisa Nomura
I：岡本よしろう　Yoshiro Okamoto　Web Designer：平山智也　Tomoya Hirayama
DF, SB：野村デザイン制作室　NOMURA DESIGN FACTORY
Printing：大村印刷　Omura Printing Co., Ltd.　Japan

山口県立美術館
「興福寺国宝展 −鎌倉復興期のみほとけ−」
興福寺国宝シール

Yamaguchi Prefectural Art Museum " National Treasures of
Kofukuji from the Temple Revival of Kamakura Period"

美術館　Art Museum

仏像をかたどったシールは、仏像の特徴が捉えやすいようにサイズや
加工が工夫されている。また、「こども興福寺豆書状」と名付けられた
台紙は、シールを全部集めなければ埋まらない、コレクターや子ども
心をくすぐる楽しいアイテムとなっている。

The Buddha stickers were designed in terms of size and manufacture to show the special nature of Buddha in an easy-to-
understand way. The idea of stickers was adopted as a means of
encouraging museum visitors to observe the detail of Buddha
that ordinarily they would not notice and also to create new Buddha devotees. You have to collect all the stickers to fill up the
special Kids ' Kofukuji Temple sticker album. Something fun to
do that will delight collectors and kids alike.

配布対象:山口県内全小中学生・来館者　**配布方法・場所:**小中学校・美術館内・
美術館周辺のお店　**狙い・効果:**シールにすることで普段はあまり気にとめな
い仏像の細部にまで目を向けさせるというねらいもあり、新たな仏像ファンの
獲得に一役買っている

Target market: Primary and middle school students and visitors to the
Museum from throughout Yamaguchi Prefecture
Distribution method and area: Primary and middle schools, at the
Museum and at stores in the vicinity of the Museum
Aim and effect: A seal was chosen in order to get visitors to observe the
detail of the Buddhist image that they ordinarily would not notice and to
create new fans.

CL：山口県立美術館 Yamaguchi Prefectural Art Museum
AD, D：野村勝久 Katsuhisa Nomura　D：石田暁子 Akiko Ishida
CW：大賀郁子 Ikuko Oga　Web Designer：平山智也 Tomoya Hirayama
DF, SB：野村デザイン制作室 NOMURA DESIGN FACTORY
Printing：大村印刷 Omura Printing Co., Ltd.　Japan

山口県立美術館 「ウィーン美術アカデミー名品展 ヨーロッパ絵画の400年」告知用パスポート

Yamaguchi Prefectural Art Museum
" Great Works from the Academy of Fine Arts Vienna – European paintings for 400 years "

美術館 Art Museum

展覧会会場へ入ること自体をウィーン旅行に見立てて作成された「美術館旅券」は、表紙や中身のレイアウトはもちろんのこと、ハンコのにじみや地紋に至るまで、本物のパスポートのようにデザインされている。また、よりリアルな疑似体験ができるように、会場で実際に入国・出国のハンコを押せるようにした。

The "art museum passport " designed to simulate an actual visit to Vienna upon entering the exhibition hall was designed to look exactly like a genuine passport, from the layout of the cover and the inside pages to the slight blurring of the stamps. To make the simulated experience even more realistic, the passport is stamped with an entry and exit stamp as you enter and leave the exhibition hall. The passport was hugely successful in attracting visitors to the exhibition.

配布対象：山口県内全小中学生・来館者　配布方法・場所：小中学校・美術館内・美術館周辺のお店
狙い・効果：子どもが海外旅行の疑似体験として楽しめたため、親子での来館者が増加した
Target market : Primary and middle school students and visitors to the Museum from throughout Yamaguchi Prefecture　**Distribution method and area :** Primary and middle schools and stores in the vicinity of the Museum
Aim and effect : Because the children enjoyed the simulated experience of overseas travel, the number of family groups visiting the Museum increased.

CL—山口県立美術館 Yamaguchi Prefectural Art Museum　AD, D：野村勝久 Katsuhisa Nomura
Web Designer：平山智也 Tomoya Hirayama　DF, SB：野村デザイン制作室 NOMURA DESIGN FACTORY
Printing：大村印刷 Omura Printing Co., Ltd.　Japan

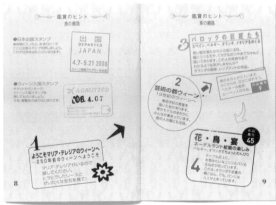

島根県立石見美術館 「なつかしの風景 大下藤次郎の水彩画」スティックガーデン

IWAMI ART MUSEUM
"Landscapes from times past - The Watercolors of Tojiro Oshita" Stick Garden

美術館 Art Museumt

自然を水彩で描き続けた大下藤次郎のエコロジーなイメージを出すためのツールとして「スティックガーデン（しおり状の台紙に水溶性のシールで種がパックされており、土に差し込んで水を与えれば発芽する）」を制作。台紙も大下藤次郎の描く世界観を大切にしたやわらかいデザインに仕上がっている。

The stick gardens (seeds packaged on a narrow rectangular cardboard base with water-soluble seals, that will germinate when planted in the ground and watered) were produced to convey the ecological aspect of the work of Tojiro Oshita who painted scenes from nature in watercolors. Because with the stick garden, the cardboard base is planted in the ground, the purpose was to bring back memories of the exhibition whenever people tended their plants. The cardboard base is of a soothing design that shows an appreciation for Tojiro Oshita's view on life.

配布対象：展覧会の来館者（前期・後期両方の観覧者）　配布方法・場所：美術館
狙い・効果：植物を世話するたびに展覧会のことを思い出してもらえること・前期と後期への来館
Target market : Visitors to the exhibition (Both the first half and the latter harf of the exhibition period.)
Distribution method and area : Art museum　**Aim and effect :** To bring back memories of the exhibition whenever someone is tending plants.

CL：島根県立石見美術館 IWAMI ART MUSEUM　AD, D：野村勝久 Katsuhisa Nomura
DF, SB：野村デザイン制作室 NOMURA DESIGN FACTORY
Printing：大村印刷 Omura Printing Co., Ltd.　Japan

トヨタ自動車「iQ MUSEUM」
アートブックプレゼントキャンペーン
Toyota Motor Corporation "iQ Museum":
Art book gift campaign

自動車メーカー Auto manufacture

従来のサイズの概念を打破することを目指し、トヨタより発売された
マイクロプレミアムカー「iQ」の魅力を紹介したアートブック。5人の有
名アーティストが「iQ」とコラボレーションしたビジュアル作品を公式サ
イトに掲載。それらの作品を一冊にまとめ、キャンペーンサイトからの
応募により、抽選で5000名にプレゼントされた。

An art book that introduces the charm of the micro-premium car iQ released
by Toyota, the aim of which was to do away with concepts of a conventional
size for motor vehicles. Visual works that are the product of a collaboration
between five famous artists and iQ were uploaded to the official site. The
visuals were combined into a book and presented to 5,000 people selected
by lottery who entered the draw on the campaign website.

配布対象：プレゼント応募者　配布方法・場所：郵送　制作数：5,000
Target market：People who entered for the campaign gift
Distribution method and area：Mail　Number produced：5,000

CL, SB：トヨタ自動車 TOYOTA MOTOR CORPORATION
CD：大山秀雄（日本デザインセンター） Hideo Ohyama (Nippon Design Center, Inc.)
AD：藤原奈緒（日本デザインセンター） Nao Fujiwara (Nippon Design Center, Inc.)
P [4, 69 / 6-9 / 17-19 / 45 / 19-50L]：
遠藤 匡（日本デザインセンター） Tadashi Endo (Nippon Design Center, Inc.)
P [13-15]：宮原康弘（アキューブ） Yasuhiro Miyahara (acube inc.)
P [16]：木奥恵三 Keizo Kioku　P [21-23]：塚田直寛 Naohiro Tsukada (STASH)
P [24-25]：河野政人 Masato Kawano (Nacása & Partners Inc.)
P [26-27]：池田晶紀（ゆかい） Masanori Ikeda (Yukai)
P [29-35]：椎木俊介 Shunsuke Shiinoki (TOUNOKI CO.,LTD)
P [46-48 / 50R-51]：シンヤケイタ Keita Shinya (ROLLUPstudio.)
CW：上野 晃（日本デザインセンター） Akira Ueno (Nippon Design Center, Inc.)
Agency：デルフィス Delphys Inc.　Japan

AZUMA MAKOTO PRIVATE GALLERY
" AMPP " vol. 14

ギャラリー・出版 Gallery・Publication

気鋭のフラワーアーティスト東 信がオープンさせた「AZUMA MAKOTO
PRIVATE GALLERY（AMPG）」。1ヶ月ごとに展示が変わるAMPG
に合わせて制作される「AMPP」は、展示が完成する制作工程を伝える
内容となっており、アーティストの作品のパワーをできる限りストレー
トに感じてもらえるようなデザインに仕上がっている。

Azuma Makoto Private Gallery (AMPG) opened by the energetic
floral artist, Azuma Makoto. AMPP, produced as a complement to
AMPG where the exhibitions change on a monthly basis, relates
the production process culminating in an exhibition and is designed to make you feel in as direct a way as possible the power of
the work produced by the artists.

CL：Cookie Publisher　AD, SB：浜田武士 Takeshi Hamada
P：Shunsuke Shiinoki　Printing：インサイド INSIDE
Artist：東 信 Makoto Azuma　Japan

PRGR 顧客ノベルティ
PRGR : Customer novelty

ゴルフメーカー Golf products manufacturer

試打会に来てくれた顧客や商品を購入してくれた人にプレゼントする、ティーとゴルフボール。イラストレーターの大塚いちお氏が描いたイラストは「happy Golf」を呼びかけ、見る人にゴルフがしたくなる気持ちを起こさせる絵柄となっており、ポスターやカタログにも同コンセプトの絵柄がおとしこまれている。

Tea and a golf ball presented to customers who attended the hit-out session. The illustration by illustrator, Ichio Otsuka was called "Happy Golf" and designed to make the people who see it feel the urge to play golf. A design with a similar concept was used for the poster and the catalogue.

配布対象：顧客　配布方法・場所：試打会・店頭
Target market : Customers
Distribution method and area : Hit-out session, Stores

CL：横浜ゴム THE YOKOHAMA RUBBER CO., LTD.
CD：金尾泰雄 Yasuo Kanao　AD：永井裕明 Hiroaki Nagai
D：藤井 圭 Kei Fujii　I：大塚いちお Ichio Otsuka
CW：瀬戸忠保 Tadayasu Seto　Agency：コモンズ COMMONS CO., LTD.
DF, SB：エヌ・ジー N.G. INC.　Japan

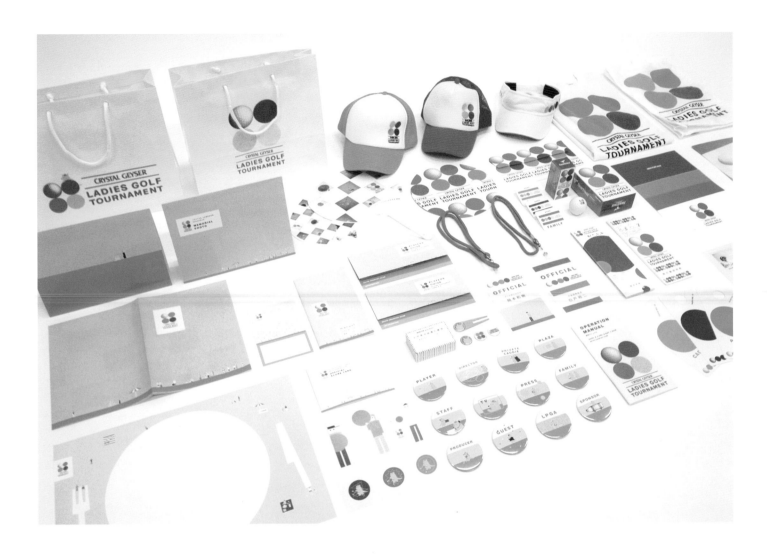

クリスタルガイザー
「レディスゴルフトーナメント」ツール

Crystal Geyser "Ladies Golf Tournament":
Promotional Tools

ゴルフ大会 Golf competitions

ゴルフトーナメントの開催にあたり、製作されたツールの数々。ロゴの4つのサークルはそれぞれ意味が異なり、ピンクは女の子らしさ、グリーンはゴルフ場、ブルーはクリスタルガイザーを表している。スタッフが使用するキャップやTシャツ、うちわなどのツールはロゴをポイントとしたデザインに。缶バッジやステッカーなど一般客に配られるツールには、親しみやすいカンガルーのキャラクターが施されている。

A range of promotional items produced for the holding of a golf tournament. Each of the four circles on the logo has a special meaning: the color pink expresses femininity, green the golf course and blue, the crystal geyser. The logo is the key design element of the items that include caps, T-shirts and fans used by Crystal Geyser staff. The items including the metal badges and stickers distributed to the general clientele incorporate a friendly kangaroo character.

配布対象：関係者・来場者 配布方法・場所：ゴルフトーナメント会場
狙い・効果：デザインの力で、女子ゴルフをよりポップな印象に変えた
Target market : Related persons, visitors to the golf course
Distribution method and area : Golf tournament venue
Aim and effect : The image of women's golf was turned into something more "pop" through the power of design.

CL：大塚ビバレジ / クリスタルガイザーレディスゴルフトーナメント
　　Otsuka Beverage Co., Ltd. / CRYSTAL GEYSER LADIES GOLF TOURNAMENT
CD, AD：佐野研二郎 Kenjiro Sano   D, I：小杉幸一 Koichi Kosugi
D：岡本和樹 Kazuki Okamoto / 原野賢太郎 Kentaro Harano
SB：MR_DESIGN   Japan

a

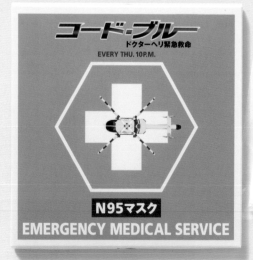

コード・ブルー
ドクターヘリ緊急救命
EVERY THU. 10P.M.

N95マスク
EMERGENCY MEDICAL SERVICE

b

3M 9010
Particulate Respirator N95
Respirateur N95 contre
les particules
Respirador contra partículas N95

フジテレビ新番組ノベルティ
Fuji Television : Novelties for new TV program

放送局 Broadcast

フジテレビの新番組「エチカの鏡」、「コード・ブルー」の宣伝用ノベルティ。「エチカの鏡」は「ココロにキクテレビ」というキャッチコピーから、処方箋をモチーフにしたパッケージの中にキャンディを入れて配布した。「コード・ブルー」はドクターヘリの緊急救命がテーマのドラマであることから、オリジナルパッケージに入った「N95マスク（微粒子除去用マスク）」を制作した。

A novelty to promote the new programs "Ethica's Mirror" and "Code Blue." For "Ethica's Mirror," packs of candy with a pharmaceutical prescription motif were distributed based on the catch copy of "television to heal your soul." An N95 mask, for filtering out fine particles, was produced in original packaging to complement a drama about the life-saving rescue operations of a helicopter paramedics team in "Code Blue."

配布対象：関係者・視聴者　配布方法・場所：手渡し・郵送
制作数：[a] 500個・[b] 1,300個
Target market : Related persons, viewers
Distribution method and area : Hand delivery, mail
Number produced : [a] 500・[b] 1,300

CL, SB：フジテレビ　Fuji Television Network, Inc.
SB [a]：鈴木文太郎（フジテレビ広告宣伝部）Buntaro Suzuki（Public relations office）　SB [b]：福田佳代（フジテレビ広告宣伝部）Kayo Fukuda（Public relations office）　Japan

フジテレビ
「ちょっぴりハッピー きっかけは、フジテレビ」
Fuji Television : "Feeling a little happy. The reason is Fuji TV."

放送局 Broadcast

「広げよう、ちょっぴりハッピー！フジテレビからあなたへ、あなたからも誰か(何か)へ」をテーマに行われたキャンペーン。ロゴは、黄色と白を基調とした、びっくり箱のようなデザインに。ペンケースやクリアファイルなどのグッズを製作した。

A campaign based on the theme "Feeling a little happy. Let's spread it around! From Fuji TV to you and from you to someone (or something) else." The yellow and white logo has a jack-in-the-box-style design. Goods including pen case and clear files were produced for the campaign.

配布対象：プレゼントキャンペーン応募者　配布方法・場所：抽選
制作数：[a] 1,000個・[b, c] 5,000個
Target market : People requesting the campaign gifts
Distribution method and area : Lottery　**Number produced :** [a] 1,000・[b, c] 5,000

CL：フジテレビジョン　Fuji Television Network, Inc.
CD：川植浩治　Kouji Kawaue　AD：池田享史　Takafumi Ikeda
D：菅 渉宇　Sho Suga / 阿閉高尚　Takahisa Atsuji　I：三好章弘　Akihiro Miyoshi
CW：藤城敦子　Atsuko Fujishiro　Planner：大宮エリー　Eri Omiya
DF, SB：デザインサービス　design service　Japan

b

クリアファイル　Clear file (a)

c

フジテレビ
「Have Your Measure
きっかけは、フジテレビ」
Fuji Television : "Have your measure.
The reason is Fuji TV."

放送局 Broadcast

「自分の物差し(Measure)を持って、もう一度世の中を見つめ直そう！」というテーマを掲げたキャンペーン。キャンペーン名の「Measure」をデザインソースに用いた楽しいデザインで、Tシャツやタオルを製作した。

Campaign based on the theme "Using your own tape measure, let's look at the world again." Fun T-shirts and towels were produced using the word "measure" in the campaign name as part of the design.

配布対象：プレゼントキャンペーン応募者　配布方法・場所：抽選
制作数：[a] 500枚・[b] 1,000枚
Target market : People requesting the campaign gifts
Distribution method and area : Lottery
Number produced : [a] 500・[b] 1,000

CL：フジテレビジョン　Fuji Television Network, Inc.
CD：川植浩治　Kouji Kawaue　AD：池田享史　Takafumi Ikeda
D：野間真吾　Shingo Noma / 高尾元樹　Motoki Takao
CW：藤城敦子　Atsuko Fujishiro
DF, SB：デザインサービス　design service　Japan

a

b

フジテレビ「サザエさん」放送40周年記念ノベルティ
Fuji Television : "Sazae-san" 40th anniversary commemorative novelty

放送局 Broadcast

1969年10月5日に放送が始まったアニメの「サザエさん」が2008年秋に放送40周年の大きな節目を迎えるにあたり、制作されたクリアファイルと紙袋。サザエさんの顔のシルエットをロゴのように大きく配置し、オレンジと茶色でシンプルにデザインしたグッズは、関係者や視聴者にプレゼントされた。

The clear files and paper bags produced to celebrate the important milestone of 40 years in the autumn of 2008 of the animation series "Sazae-san" that first aired on 5 October 1969. The goods that feature a large silhouette of Sazae-san's face used as a kind of logo and a simple design of orange and brown were presented to related people and viewers.

配布対象：関係者・視聴者　配布方法・場所：手渡し・郵送　制作数：[a] 800個・[b] 5,000個
Target market : Related persons, viewers　**Distribution method and area :** Hand delivery, mail　**Number produced :** [a] 800・[b] 5,000

CL, SB: フジテレビ Fuji Television Network, Inc.　SB: 末松千鶴（フジテレビ広告宣伝部）Chizuru Suematsu (Public relations office)
Japan

クリアファイル Clear file（a）

b

フジテレビ「子犬のラフちゃん」ノベルティ
Fuji Television : "The puppy called Rafu-chan" novelty

放送局 Broadcast

フジテレビのオリジナルキャラクター「子犬のラフちゃん」の卓上カレンダー。エコをテーマに制作されているため、各月のページに「地球温暖化を考えよう」、「マイ箸・マイコップを持とう」など、エコの勧めが書かれている。

A desk calendar featuring the original Fuji Television character, the puppy, Rafu-chan. As the calendar was produced with an ecological theme, the page for each month contains a piece of advice relating to ecology such as "Stop and think about global warming," and "Buy your own set of reusable chopsticks and cup."

配布対象：関係者・視聴者　配布方法・場所：手渡し・郵送　制作数：6,950個（うち150個は販売した）
Target market : Related persons, viewers　**Distribution method and area :** Hand delivery, mail
Number produced : 6,950（150 were for sale）

CL, SB: フジテレビ Fuji Television Network, Inc.
SB: 末松千鶴（フジテレビ広告宣伝部）Chizuru Suematsu (Public relations office)　Japan

井上ジョー 1st ミニ・アルバム 「IN A WAY」プレスキット

Inoue Joe : First mini album "IN A WAY" press kit

レコード会社 Record producer

作詞・作曲からアレンジ、すべての楽器演奏までこなすLA生まれの日本人アーティスト・井上ジョーが2007年にリリースした1stシングル「IN A WAY」のプレスキット。アーティストの「ライフスタイル」と「楽曲」を、写真とグラフィックで紹介したガイドブックで、デビューCDのプロモーションとして製作された。

A press kit for "IN A WAY," the first single, released in 2007, by Japanese artist, Inoue Joe. Born in Los Angeles, Inoue writes songs and plays a wide range of musical instruments. A guidebook that introduces the artist's lifestyle and music using photographs and graphics was produced to promote his debut single.

配布対象：業界関係者　制作数：3,000個
狙い・効果：デビューCDのプロモーション
Target market : Industry-related people　**Number produced :** 3,000
Aim and effect : Promotion of the debut CD

CL：キューンレコード　Ki/oon Record
AD, D：いのうえよしひろ ＋ yukinko　Yoshihiro Inoue ＋ yukinko
P：Daisuke Miura　DF, SB：ジョット・グラフィカ　Giottographica
Printing：ソニーミュージック コミュニケーションズ　Sony Music
Communications Inc.　Japan

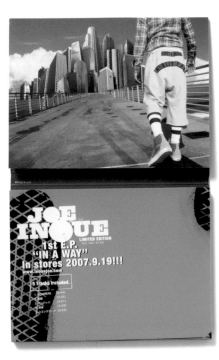

毛皮族 DVD 発売記念ノベルティ
Kegawa-zoku : Novelty to commemorate a DVD release

劇団 Theatre group

2000年9月に結成された劇団「毛皮族」のDVD発売を記念して製作された缶バッジ、Tシャツ、ティッシュボックスなどのノベルティグッズ各種。Tシャツは女性が着ると胸の部分に「d」と「☆」が重なるようになっている。また、「毛皮族★DVD」のパッケージにはバーコ印刷により本物の毛が貼り付いているかのような加工が施されている。

A range of novelties that includes metal badges, T-shirts and tissue boxes produced to commemorate a DVD release by the Kegawazoku theatrical company formed in September 2000. When women wear the T-shirt, the "d" and the "☆" cover their chests. The packaging for the Kegawa-zoku★DVD was made to feel like a real fur covering using a thermo-graphic printing process.

CL：毛皮族 Kegawa-zoku　CD：江本純子 Junko Emoto
AD：佐野研二郎 Kenjiro Sano　D：榮 良太 Ryota Sakae
SB：MR_DESIGN　Japan

DVD「FREEDOM」予約特典キャンペーン
"FREEDOM" on DVD : Pre-order special gift campaign

映像コンテンツ　Audio-visual contents

テレビCM（日清カップヌードル）から生まれたアニメーション作品「FREEDOM」のDVD予約特典としてプレゼントされた缶バッジ。全20種類あり、主要キャラクターの絵柄も全て異なるため、コレクター心に強く訴えるノベルティーとなった。

Metal badges presented to customers who pre-ordered the animated film "FREEDOM" that was spun off from the Nissin instant noodles TV commercial. The badges were available in 20 varieties and the design of each of the main characters was different, something that would strongly appeal to people who are fond of collecting.

配布対象：DVD予約購入者　配布方法・場所：店頭　狙い・効果：販売促進
Target market : Customers who pre-ordered the DVD
Distribution method and area : Stores　**Aim and effect :** Promotion of sales.

CL：バンダイビジュアル BANDAI VISUAL CO., LTD.
CD：高松 聡 Satoshi Takamatsu　CD, AD：野尻大作 Daisaku Nojiri
D：安達明日香 Asuka Adachi　CW：渡辺潤平 Junpei Watanabe
DF, SB：ground　Japan

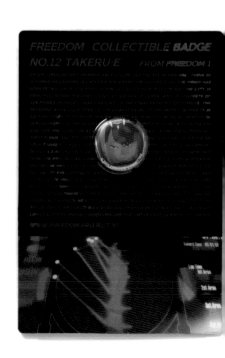

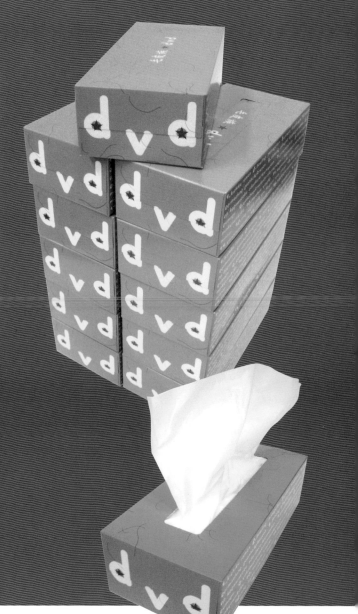

FREEDOM COLLECTIBLE BADGE
NO.16/TITLE-D FROM FREEDOM 1

IN THE 23RD CENTURY, HUMANS HAVE COLONIZED THE MOON AND ARE LIVING IN A DOMED MEGALOPOLIS CALLED EDEN WHERE THE REPUBLIC OF THE MOON HAS BEEN ESTABLISHED. THE POPULATION IS ABOUT THREE MILLION AND THE CITY IS PEACEFUL ALTHOUGH VERY CLOSELY CONTROLLED. EDEN, WHICH CONSISTS OF SIX DOMES IN HUGE LUNAR CRATERS, IS THE FINAL RETREAT OF HUMANS. THE RESIDENT AREA IS LOCATED AT THE LOWEST LEVEL OF THE DOMES, WHERE IT IS SAFE AND EASY TO PRODUCE OXYGEN. ARTIFICIAL FORESTS ON THE HIGHEST LEVEL REMIND PEOPLE OF THE WOODS THAT DISAPPEARED LONG AGO. HIGHWAYS RUN LIKE THE VEINS ON A LEAF AT THIS LEVEL. YOUNG DRIVERS ENJOY THESE ROADS, AND THE GOVERNMENT SUPERVISED BY GOVERNMENT HIGH BANKED CURVES. THE RACES FEATURING OFFICIALS RIDING ON A UNIQUE VEHICLE AND PASSING A UNMANNED TRAILERS WITH ROUGH CORNERS. TAKERU IS ONE OF THE BOYS WHO ENJOY RACING. HE HAS A VAGUE FEELING, BUT THERE IS A BIG HOLE IN HIS PEACEFUL LIFE. HE CAN GET EVERYTHING HE WANTS, BUT THERE IS A BIG HOLE IN HIS HEART, AND RUNNING HIS VEHICLE AT FULL THROTTLE CAN'T FILL THIS HOLE. HAVING FINISHED HIS COMPULSORY EDUCATION, TAKERU IS WAITING FOR AN APPROPRIATE JOB FROM THE GOVERNMENT. TAKERU STEPS ON THE ACCELERATOR, AND THE ENGINE ROARS AND WHINES. HE FEELS EXHILARATION AS HIS VEHICLE ROARS OFF INTO THE DISTANCE. HE HAS NO IDEA WHAT WILL HAPPEN IN THE NEXT RACE AND IN HIS LONG VACATION, AND HE CANNOT IMAGINE THAT HIS DESTINY IS ABOUT TO CHANGE.

WWW.FREEDOM-PROJECT.JP   © 2006 FREEDOM. ALL RIGHTS RESERVED.

FREEDOM COLLECTIBLE BADGE
NO.10/BISU-B FROM PREVISITED

IN THE 23RD CENTURY, HUMANS HAVE COLONIZED THE MOON AND ARE LIVING IN A DOMED MEGALOPOLIS CALLED EDEN WHERE THE REPUBLIC OF THE MOON HAS BEEN ESTABLISHED. THE POPULATION IS ABOUT THREE MILLION AND THE CITY IS PEACEFUL ALTHOUGH VERY CLOSELY CONTROLLED. EDEN, WHICH CONSISTS OF SIX DOMES IN HUGE LUNAR CRATERS, IS THE FINAL RETREAT OF HUMANS. THE RESIDENT AREA IS LOCATED AT THE LOWEST LEVEL OF THE DOMES, WHERE IT IS SAFE AND EASY TO PRODUCE OXYGEN. ARTIFICIAL FORESTS ON THE HIGHEST LEVEL REMIND PEOPLE OF THE WOODS THAT DISAPPEARED LONG AGO. HIGHWAYS RUN LIKE THE VEINS ON A LEAF AT THIS LEVEL. YOUNG DRIVERS ENJOY THESE ROADS, AND THE GOVERNMENT SUPERVISED BY GOVERNMENT HIGH BANKED CURVES. THE RACES FEATURING OFFICIALS RIDING ON A UNIQUE VEHICLE AND PASSING A UNMANNED TRAILERS WITH ROUGH CORNERS. TAKERU IS ONE OF THE BOYS WHO ENJOY RACING. HE HAS A VAGUE FEELING, BUT THERE IS A BIG HOLE IN HIS HEART, AND RUNNING HIS VEHICLE AT FULL THROTTLE CAN'T FILL THIS HOLE. HAVING FINISHED HIS COMPULSORY EDUCATION, TAKERU IS WAITING FOR AN APPROPRIATE JOB FROM THE GOVERNMENT. TAKERU STEPS ON THE ACCELERATOR, AND THE ENGINE ROARS AND WHINES. HE FEELS EXHILARATION AS HIS VEHICLE ROARS OFF INTO THE DISTANCE. HE HAS NO IDEA WHAT WILL HAPPEN IN THE NEXT RACE AND IN HIS LONG VACATION, AND HE CANNOT IMAGINE THAT HIS DESTINY IS ABOUT TO CHANGE.

WWW.FREEDOM-PROJECT.JP   © 2006 FREEDOM. COMMITTEE. ALL RIGHTS RESERVED

YUKI アルバム「FIVE STAR」
初回限定盤ノベルティ

Yuki : "Five Star" first limited edition album novelty

レコード会社 Record company

ソロ活動5周年を記念して制作されたアルバム。初回限定盤はボックス入りとなっており、5つの星にはシルバーレインボーの箔押しが施されている。特典の写真集の表紙や中面にも金の箔押しが施され、特別感を高めるデザインとなっている。

An album produced in commemoration of the fifth anniversary of becoming a solo artist. The first limited edition album is inside a box, with five gold stars and silver rainbow foil. Gold foil has been used here and there on the special photographic collection to enhance the idea of the special nature of the novelty.

配布対象：アルバム購入者 配布方法・場所：店頭
Target Market : Purchasers of the album
Distribution method and areat : Stores

CL：EPICレコードジャパン Epic Records Japan Inc.
AD, SB：スルー THROUGH. Japan

マグネット Magnet

flumpool デビューミニアルバム「Unreal」プレスキット＆初回限定盤

flumpool debut mini-album, "Unreal": Press kit and first limited edition album

レコード会社 Record company

2008年10月にメジャーデビューしたflumpool。デビューミニアルバム「Unreal」のプレスキットは、ミニアルバムのサンプルやメンバー4人の裸のステッカーを同封し、真空パックのパッケージに入れて郵送。受け取った人に強いインパクト与え、話題を喚起させるプレスキットにした。デビューミニアルバム「Unreal」の初回限定盤には、48ページの写真集が付いている。

The press kit for flumpool, which made its major debut in October 2008, contains a sample of the mini-album and new single, and a visual of the four members of the group naked. The press kit was vacuum-packed and mailed out. In accordance with the group's intention to create "something a little different," the press kit was designed to make a strong impact on its recipients. A full-color photo collection comes with the first limited edition of the album.

配布対象：マスコミ関係者・初回限定盤購入者　配布方法・場所：郵送・店頭　狙い・効果：購買促進
Target market : Media-related persons, purchasers of the first limited edition of the album　**Distribution method and area :** Mail, at stores　**Aim and effect :** Promotion of sales

CL：エースケッチ A-Sketch Inc.　CD, AD：長島 慎 Shin Nagashima　PL, I：石下佳奈子 Kanako Ishioroshi　D：名和田 剛 Go Nawata／数見友紀 Yuki Kazumi／齋藤若菜 Wakana Saito／小林 愛 Ai Kobayashi　P：鳥巣佑有子 Yuko Torisu　Retouch：宮本 准 Hitoshi Miyamoto　Agency, SB：博報堂 HAKUHODO Inc.
DF：アドソルト ADSALT Inc.　Japan

デジタルアートフェスティバル東京 2008
イベントグッズ

Digital Art Festival Tokyo 2008 : Event goods

番組・映像制作 Audio-visual production

「コミュニケーション」をテーマとした、インタラクティブ・アート作品「COTO-TAMA（コトタマ）」。この「COTO-TAMA」という、ルールをもった新しい言語をデザインし、キービジュアルとしてフライヤー、携帯ストラップ、Tシャツなど様々な媒体におとし込んだ。それぞれのツールは、11色の円を配した楽しいデザインとなっている。

Interactive art work, Coto-Tama, featuring the theme of communication. A new language called Coto-Tama with certain rules has been designed and as key visuals, a flyer, a mobile carry-strap and T-shirt have been made using various media. Each of the tools has a fun design consisting of arrangements of nine differently colored circles.

配布対象：来場者・関係者　**狙い・効果**：イベント会場のイメージ・統一感のアップ
Target market : Visitors to the festival, related persons　**Aim and effect** : Enhance the image of the event, increase the sense of consistency

CL：NHKエンタープライズ NHK ENTERPRISES, INC.　CD：大八木 翼 Tsubasa Oyagi
AD, D：小杉幸一 Koichi Kosugi　Agency, SB：博報堂 HAKUHODO Inc.
Printing：日光プロセス Nikko Process Co., Ltd.　Japan

フライヤー　Flyer

「人のセックスを笑うな」
初回限定DVD

First limited edition DVD
"Hito no sekkusu-wo warau na"
(Don't Laugh at my Romance)

DVDメーカー　DVD manufacture

映画「人のセックスを笑うな」初回限定DVD購入者限定のプレゼントキャンペーンとして製作されたノベルティ。コアユーザーに初回盤を購入してもらうための販売促進用として、劇中でセットの一部として置かれていたロバの人形をミニチュア・フィギュア化したものを、キャンペーンに応募した人の中から抽選で100名にプレゼントした。

A novelty produced for a gift campaign limited to purchasers of the first release DVD of the film "Don't Laugh at my Romance". The 100 winners determined by lottery were presented with a miniature version of the toy donkeys that were placed around as part of the set during screenings, as a means of promoting sales by getting fans to buy the DVD.

狙い・効果：購買促進　**Aim and effect** : Sales promotion

CL, SB：ハピネット　Happinet Corporation　Japan

「マイ・ブルーベリー・ナイツ」プレミアムBOX

"My Blueberry Nights": Premium Box

映画配給　Film distribution

映画に登場する二人の恋が始まるきっかけとなるブルーベリー・パイと、高級なスイーツの入った
小箱をイメージしてデザインされた外箱は「女性たちにスイーツを買う時のようにワクワクしながら
買って欲しい」との思いが込められている。箱の中にはDVDのほか、監督自ら撮影したフォトブック、
ポスター、ブックレットなど、いくつもの特典が収められている。

The packaging was designed upon the idea of the blueberry pie that brought about the love
affair between the two protagonists in the film and the small boxes that contain high-quality
sweets, the aim being to produce the kind of excitement that young women experience when
they go sweet shopping. There are several other special surprises inside the box in addition
to the DVD, including a book of photos taken by the director himself, a poster and a booklet.

狙い・効果：購買促進　Aim and effect：Sales promotion

CL, CD, SB：アスミック・エース エンタテインメント　Asmik Ace Entertainment, Inc.
D：吉川俊彰（アブソリュート グラマー）　Toshiaki Yoshikawa (absolute GLAMOUR)
DF：アブソリュート グラマー　absolute GLAMOUR　Printing：久栄社　Kyueisha
Printing（Box）：博進紙器　HAKUSHIN-SHIKI Co., Ltd.　Japan

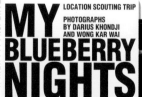

「赤い風船 / 白い馬 ［デジタルニューマスター］」2枚組 初回限定生産スーベニア・ボックス

"Digitally re-mastered The Red Balloon /
White Mane" : Two disc limited edition box set

映画配給 Film distribution

'56 カンヌ国際映画祭パルム・ドール受賞『赤い風船』、'53 同映画祭グランプリ受賞『白い馬』の2枚組DVD初回生産スーベニア・ボックス。パリの雑貨をイメージし、世代を超えて長く愛されることを意識してデザインされている。中にはDVDをはじめ、劇場で使われたフィルムの切り出し、ポストカード、特製ブックレット等が封入されている。

A never-seen-before souvenir box set containing two films: The Red Balloon, winner of the Palme d'Or, and White Mane, winner of the Grand Prix at the Cannes Film Festival. The design, with its Parisian flavor, seeks to make these films favorites for many generations to come. Inside are DVDs of the films, cuts used at theaters, postcards etc.

狙い・効果：作品の昔からのファンに対しては、古い名作が新たにDVDで甦ることをアピールし、手元に持っていたいと思ってもらえることを目指した。新たなファン層に対しては、色褪せない魅力をもつ映画であることを伝えられるパッケージを意識した

Aim and effect : The films has been designed to convey the never-diminishing charm of the films.

CL, CD, SB：アスミック・エース エンタテインメント　Asmik Ace Entertainment, Inc.
D：大寿美トモエ　Tomoe Osumi　DF：大寿美デザイン　Osumi Design
Printing：久栄社　Kyueisha　Printing（Box）：博進紙器　HAKUSHIN-SHIKI Co., Ltd.　Japan

「大人たばこ養成講座
新成人のお作法2008」
プレゼントキャンペーン

"Otona Tobacco Training Course - Etiquette
for new grown-ups 2008"
gift campaign Cigarettes

たばこ　Cigarettes

人気広告シリーズ「大人たばこ養成講座」の第84弾。「新成人のお作法」と題し、14項目の作法をイラストとコピーでおもしろおかしく綴っている。「時には大人もはじけたい」というわけで、フランス産特製シャンパン「シュワらしき人生」のプレゼントキャンペーンを行った。当選者には、「大人たばこ養成講座」の登場人物が箔押しされた、オリジナルのラベルがついたシャンパンがプレゼントされる。

Number 84 of the popular advertising series. Titled "Etiquette for new grown-ups," the fourteen pieces of etiquette advice make interesting and humorous use of illustration and copy. The special French champagne "Live a Sparkling Wonderful Life!" campaign was launched with the idea that "sometimes grown-ups also need to sparkle like champagne."

配布対象：プレゼント応募者　配布方法・場所：郵送
制作数：1,000個
Target market : Persons who request the campaign gift
Distribution method and area : Mail
Number produced : 1,000

CL：日本たばこ産業　JAPAN TOBACCO INC.
AD：寄藤文平　Bunpei Yorifuji
CW：岡本欣也　Kinya Okamoto
Agency, SB：博報堂　HAKUHODO Inc.　Japan

the chef cooks me アルバム
「ライフスタイル・メイクスマイル
コンパクトディスク」
プレスキット

the chef cooks me : "lifestyle make smile"
CD press kit

レコード会社 Record company

the chef cooks meのプレスキットは、バンド名が「食」を
連想させることからピザのパッケージにサンプルCDを入
れ、リーフレットとともに郵送した。リーフレットは、メ
ニュー表のようなデザインとし、メンバーのプロフィール
やディスコグラフィーを掲載。届くと思わず開けてしまう、
楽しいプレスキットに仕上げた。

The press kit for the chef cooks me contained a sample CD packaged in a pizza box to make the association with food in the band's name, and was mailed out
together with a leaflet. The leaflet was designed to
resemble a restaurant menu and contains profiles of
the members and a discography. The press kit is fun
and impossible to resist opening.

配布対象：マスコミ関係者 配布方法・場所：郵送
Target Market : Media-related persons
Distribution method and area : Mail

CL：エスエムイーレコーズ SME Records Inc.
CD, AD：長島 慎 Shin Nagashima D：内田 翔 Sho Uchida
P：薄井一議 Kazuyoshi Usui Agency, SB：博報堂
HAKUHODO Inc. DF：Sude Sude ltd. Japan

レッドバロン新卒採用活動・インターンシップ 参加記念ノベルティ

Novelty for RED BARON new graduate recruitment / internship commemoration

オートバイ販売 Motorcycle sales

入社を希望する学生のほとんどがライダーであるということに着目し、交通安全と就職祈願のお守りを作成。道路とネクタイをモチーフにしたお守りは、並べるとふたつの絵が繋がるデザインになっており、「趣味のバイクと仕事が合わさったところがレッドバロン」という意味が込められている。また、「お守りらしさ」を意識した紙袋の裏面には、学生たちへのメッセージが印刷されている。

Having noticed that many of the students who applied for employment in the company were motorcycle riders, o-mamori, amulets were created to promote road safety and as a prayer for employment with the company. When the o-mamori, one with a road and the other with a business tie as their respective motifs, are placed beside each other, their designs interconnect to express the idea that "RED BARON brings together the pastime of motorcycle riding and work."

配布対象：就職活動の学生　配布方法・場所：インターンシップ会場　制作数：200個
狙い・効果：楽しいグッズから、会社の良さが伝わることを目指し作成した
Target market : Student job-seekers　**Distribution method and area :** Internship venue
Number produced : 200　**Aim and effect :** The aim was to convey the good points of the company using fun novelty goods

CL：レッドバロン　RED BARON Co., Ltd.　CD：柴田友康　Tomoyasu Shibata／日野貴行　Takayuki Hino　AD, D, I：平井秀和　Hidekazu Hirai　CW：漆畑陽生　Yousei Urushibata　Agency：リクルートメディアコミュニケーションズ　Recruit Media Communications　DF, SB：ピースグラフィックス　Peace Graphics　Japan

タワーレコード　オリジナルグッズ

TOWER RECORDS : Original goods

音楽小売 Music retail

夏フェスなど、イベント会場での携帯のキャンペーンや社会貢献活動参加者へのノベルティ。環境活動「タワエコ」グッズの帽子、マイ箸などがある。2008年「タワエコ」のデザインテーマは、「open-endedness」。人の脳の可能性のように限りなく進歩しつづけることを、スカルと若葉の輪廻転生で表現した。

Novelties designed for use at summer festivals and other events by actively contributing members of society. The novelties include the environmentally aware "Tower Eco" hat and chopsticks. The Tower Eco design theme is "open-endedness." Boundless progress and the boundless potential of the human brain are expressed with a scull and the life-to-death cycle of young leaves.

配布対象：イベント会場での携帯キャンペーンや社会貢献活動参加者
配布方法・場所：参加者に対する抽選・イベント会場内ブース
狙い・効果：キャンペーンへの参加誘引と会場での使用
Target market : Persons actively contributing to society
Distribution method and area : Lottery for participants, booth at event venues
Aim and effect : Encourage participation in the campaign and use of the goods at events.

CL, CD, SB：タワーレコード　TOWER RECORDS　D, I, DF：7STARS　Japan

「Casa BRUTUS」
名作家具ヌードペン・建築マグネット
"Casa BRUTUS" : Nude pens featuring famous furniture pieces, architecture magnets

出版 Publishing

マガジンハウス発行「Casa BRUTUS」の年間購読契約者に配られる、ヌードペンとマグネット。ヌードペンの絵柄は、名作家具がモチーフに。建築マグネットは、人や動物、木などを好きなように組み合わせて遊べる仕組みとなっており、建築・インテリア誌らしいノベルティとなっている。

A nude pen and a set of architecture magnets distributed to annual subscribers of Casa BRUTUS magazine published by Magazine House. The nude pen has a motif of famous furniture pieces and the architecture magnets are fun to arrange with people, animals and trees. The Casa BRUTUS novelties are just the right thing for an architecture and interior design magazine.

配布対象：年間購読契約者（現在は別のグッズを配布）
配布方法・場所：郵送
Target market : Annual subscribers (Different goods are currently being distributed.)　**Distribution method and area :** Mail

CL：マガジンハウス　Magazine House, Ltd.
AD, D, SB：グルーヴィジョンズ　groovisions　Japan

しおり
Bookmark

角川文庫「変装松ケン図書カード」
プレゼントキャンペーン

Kadokawa Pocket Editions : "Matsu Ken in Disguise"
prepaid card gift campaign

出版 Publishing

「発見。角川ミステリ」のキャンペーンとして、俳優の松山ケンイチ
が変装したポスターやしおりを駅や書店で展開。全部で何パターンの
変装があるかを見破り、答えを書いて応募した人の中から、抽選で
「変装松ケン図書カード」3枚セットがプレゼントされた。ビビッドな
赤と黒の2色印刷にすることで、見る人に強い印象を与えるデザイ
ンに仕上げた。

As part of the "Discovered! Kadokawa mysteries" campaign,
posters and paper wraparounds featuring the actor Kenichi
Matsuyama in various disguises were rolled out at stations and
at bookstores. The first step was to figure out what the disguises
were, then send in the answers. The winners chosen by lottery
were presented with a set of three prepaid cards for purchasing
book. The design is eye-catching, printed in the two colors of
vivid red and black.

配布対象：応募者　配布方法・場所：郵送　狙い・効果：販売促進
Target market : People who enter the competition
Distribution method and area : Mail　**Aim and effect :** Promotion of sales

CL：角川書店　Kadokawa Shoten Publishing Co., Ltd.
AD：田中 元　Gen Tanaka　Agency, SB：電通　DENTSU Inc.　Japan

ポップ P.O.P

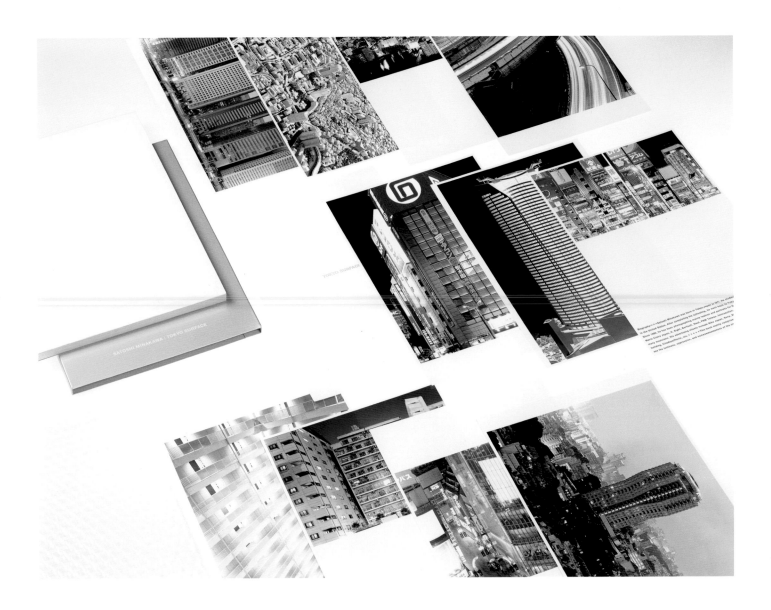

Satoshi Minakawa ポートフォリオ
Satoshi Minakawa Portfolio

写真家 Photographer

イギリスと日本を拠点に活動している写真家のポートフォリオ。銀と白の美しいボックスの中には、「TOKYO SURFACE」という作品が納められている。製本されたものではなく、1枚1枚が独立しているため、まるで本物のプリントを見ているような気持ちになる作品集となっている。

Portfolio of a photographer who is based in the UK and Japan. In the beautiful silver and white box is the work titled "TOKYO SURFACE". By keeping the photographs separate from each other and not making them into a book, this photographic collection creates a sense of looking at the real photographic prints.

配布対象：クライアント　**Target market :** Clients

CL, P：皆川 聡　Satoshi Minakawa
AD, D：野尻大作　Daisaku Nojiri　DF, SB：ground　Japan

集英社「ナツイチ」キャンペーン
Shueisha "Natsuichi" Campaign

出版 Publishing

集英社が毎夏に展開している「夏の一冊 ナツイチ」キャンペーンの販促用ノベルティ。集英社文庫が身近に感じられるようにと、同文庫のアイコンとなっている「ハチ」のキャラクターを生かし、「知的でラブリーなトーン」で統一している。読者向けには携帯ストラップをプレゼント、書店向けには日頃の業務に使用できるグッズを用意した。

A range of novelty goods created to promote sales during the "My Favorite Book this Summer" Campaign launched by Shueisha every summer. A bee character was chosen as the icon for promoting Shueisha's paperback range, and the campaign was given an "intellectual yet amiable" tone. Readers were presented with a mobile phone strap and bookstores, with a range of goods that could be used in their everyday business.

配布対象：書店・読者　配布方法・場所：書店　狙い・効果：読者向けのグッズは購入促進に、書店向けのグッズは、集英社文庫をより身近な存在として認識してもらうための店頭ディスプレイとして機能した

Target market : Bookstores, readers
Distribution method and area : Bookstores
Aim and effect : For the customers served to promote sales and those for the bookstores were used for store displays.

CL：集英社　Shueisha Inc.　CD：高崎卓馬　Takuma Takasaki
AD：居山浩二　Koji Iyama　D：赤土佳子　Yoshiko Akado / 新井かおる
Kaoru Arai　P：土井文雄　Fumio Doi　I：山田詩子　Utako Yamada
CW：太田祐美子　Yumiko Ota　Agency：電通　DENTSU INC.
DF, SB：イヤマデザイン　Iyamadesign　Japan

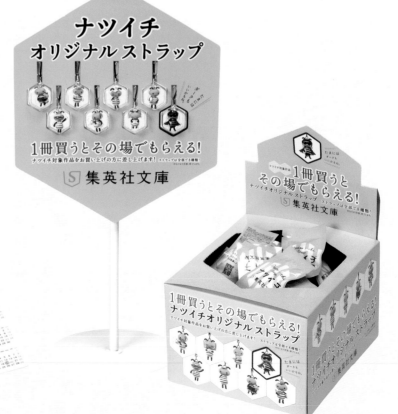

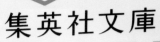

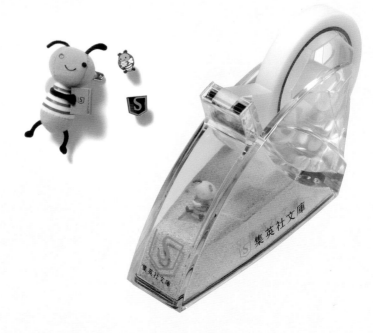

新聞 Newspaper

「昔の商人は働く知恵を心得ていた」という視点から、大阪に伝わる学ぶべき信念やアイデアを綴った、大人のための参考書、「なるほど心得綴り」を制作した。思わずうなってしまうようなユニークさもさることながら、表紙には厚い紙を使用し、ジャバラ折りの形態にするなど、日本経済新聞のイメージと「働く」ということを上手くリンクさせながら、「どこか懐かしく、質が高い」というイメージが定着するよう、細部にまでこだわってデザインされている。

A reference book for adults, that shares with Osaka the invaluable working wisdom of the Osaka merchants of olden days. The image of Nikkei Inc. has been cleverly connected to the idea of "working" with the use of heavy paper for the cover and a bellows fold etc.

配布対象：関西・西日本地区 配布方法・場所：日本経済新聞試読・購読者 狙い・効果：質の高い内容が、日本経済新聞のイメージにつながるような質感を演出した結果、きちんと保存しておきたくなるものとなった
Target market : Kansai and Western Japan
Distribution method and area : Trial readers and subscribers of Nikkei Inc **Aim and effect :** Because the high-quality content created an awareness of quality that connected to Nikkei Inc, the leaflet was something that people wanted to hold onto.

CL：日本経済新聞社大阪本社 Nikkei Inc. Osaka Head Office
CD, AD, D：野村勝久 Katsuhisa Nomura
CD, CW：大賀郁子 Ikuko Oga
Web Designer：平山智也 Tomoya Hirayama
DF, SB：野村デザイン制作室 NOMURA DESIGN FACTORY
Printing：多聞印刷 Tamon Printing Co., Ltd. Japan

「日経デザイン」250号記念
特別企画キャンペーングッズ
"Nikkei Design" : Commemoration of the 250th edition special campaign goods

出版 Publishing

「日経デザイン」創刊250号を記念して製作された封筒とタトウケース。贈り物とするにふさわしい封筒を目指し、通常は何も印刷されないのりしろ部分にも印刷が施されたことで、包装紙のようなたたずまいとなっている。封筒の中には、鮮やかな赤と緑の格子をまとめたタトウケースが入っており、付属の蓄光シールを貼ってカスタマイズできる。

Envelope and case produced to commemorate the 250th edition of Nikkei Design. The aim was to create envelopes that were suitable to present as gifts, and by printing on the seal part of the envelope on which ordinarily nothing is printed, the envelopes resemble wrapping paper. Inside the envelope is a case made from bright red and green check Japanese paper that can be customized by attaching the phosphorescent sticker that is included.

配布対象：定期購読者　配布方法・場所：郵送　制作数：15,000個
Target market : Regular subscribers　**Distribution method and area :** Mail
Number produced : 15,000

CL：日経BP　Nikkei Business Publications, Inc.
AD, D：北川一成　Issay Kitagawa　DF, Printing, SB：グラフ　GRAPH
Processing：ハグルマ封筒　HAGURUMA ENVELOPE Co., Ltd.　Japan

蓄光ステッカー　Phosphorescent stickers

特殊紙の全国プロモーション DM
Nation-wide promotional DM for special papers

紙卸業 Wholesale paper business

特殊紙のプロモーションのための印刷見本。サンプルとしてだけではなく、実際に使ってもらえるように12ヶ月分のランチョンマットを製作した。それぞれの紙の質感を活かしたデザイン、印刷となっている。

Printing samples for promotion of special papers. In addition to the samples, a luncheon mat for each month of the year that can be put into actual use was manufactured using special paper. The DM has been designed and printed to show off the quality of each of the special papers.

配布対象：全国のデザイナー　配布方法・場所：郵送
制作数：8,000個　狙い・効果：新しい印刷表現による、ファンシーペーパーのプロモーション。
Target market : Designers throughout Japan
Distribution method and area : Mail
Number produced : 8,000　**Aim and effect :** Promotion of fancy papers with new printing methods.

CL：平和紙業　Heiwa Paper Co., Ltd.　AD, D：北川一成
Issay Kitagawa　DF, Printing, SB：グラフ　GRAPH　Japan

竹尾見本帖本店
「マーメイド タグ セッション」展 ノベルティ

Takeo Mihoncho Honten Special Exhibition "Mermaid Tag Session": Exhibition novelty

紙専門商社 Specialty paper company

さざ波のような風合いを特徴とするファインペーパーの定番「マーメイド」の発売50周年を記念して開催された展覧会。新商品の「エルマーメイド」「リバーシブルマーメイド」も使用され、気鋭のクリエイター４名がそれぞれ100種類のタグを通して「マーメイド」の魅力を引き出した。

An exhibition commemorating the 50th anniversary of the release of one of Takeo's best selling fine papers, Mermaid, with its look and feel of rippling water.

配布対象：来場者　配布方法・場所：竹尾 見本帖本店２Ｆ　制作数：1,000
Target market : Visitors to the exhibition　Distribution method and area : Second floor, Takeo Mihoncho Honten　Number produced : 1,000

CL, SB：竹尾 TAKEO CO., LTD.　AD：松下計デザイン室 KEI Matsushita Design Room Inc.　D：大谷有紀（資生堂）Yuki Otani（SHISEIDO CO., LTD.）
／岡室 健 Ken Okamuro（HAKUHODO DESIGN Inc.）／ 関本明子（ドラフト）Akiko Sekimoto（Draft Co., Ltd.）／
田辺智子（松下計デザイン室）Tomoko Tanabe（KEI Matsushita Design Room Inc.）　DF：松下計デザイン室 KEI Matsushita Design Room Inc.
Printing：福寿産業 FUKUJU SANGYO CO., LTD.／日本写真印刷 Nissha Printing Co., Ltd.
Processing：舟木紙工所 Funaki paper manufacturing, Inc.／ ツジカワ Tsujikawa Co., Ltd.　Japan

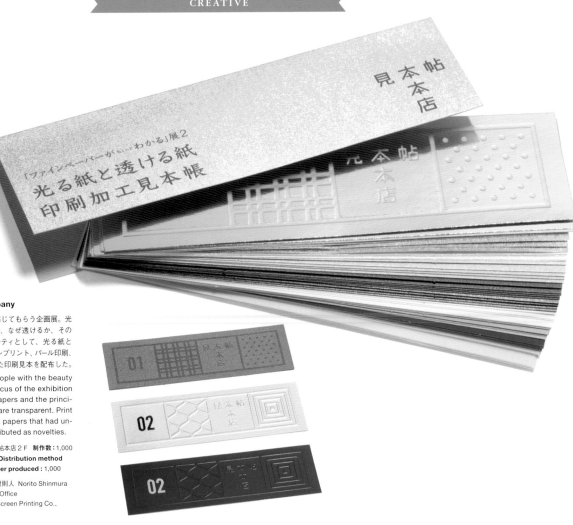

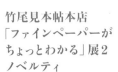

竹尾見本帖本店
「ファインペーパーが
ちょっとわかる」展2
ノベルティ

Takeo Mihoncho Honten :
"Discovering fine papers"
Exhibition 2 novelty

紙専門商社 Specialty paper company

ファインペーパーの魅力と実力を身近に感じてもらう企画展。光る紙と透ける紙を取り上げ、なぜ光るか、なぜ透けるか、その原理と製法を視覚的に紹介した。ノベルティとして、光る紙と透ける紙にシルク印刷、フラッシュビジョンプリント、パール印刷、エンボス加工、UV厚盛り印刷などを施した印刷見本を配布した。

A special exhibition to familiarize people with the beauty and the power of fine papers. The focus of the exhibition was shiny papers and transparent papers and the principles of why they shine and why they are transparent. Print samples using shiny and transparent papers that had undergone various processes were distributed as novelties.

配布対象：来場者 配布方法・場所：竹尾 見本帖本店 2 F 制作数：1,000
Target market : Visitors to the exhibition **Distribution method and area** : Visitors to the exhibition **Number produced** : 1,000

CL, SB：竹尾 TAKEO CO., LTD.　AD：新村則人 Norito Shinmura
DF：新村デザイン事務所 Shinmura Design Office
Processing：内藤プロセス Naito Process Screen Printing Co.,
Japan

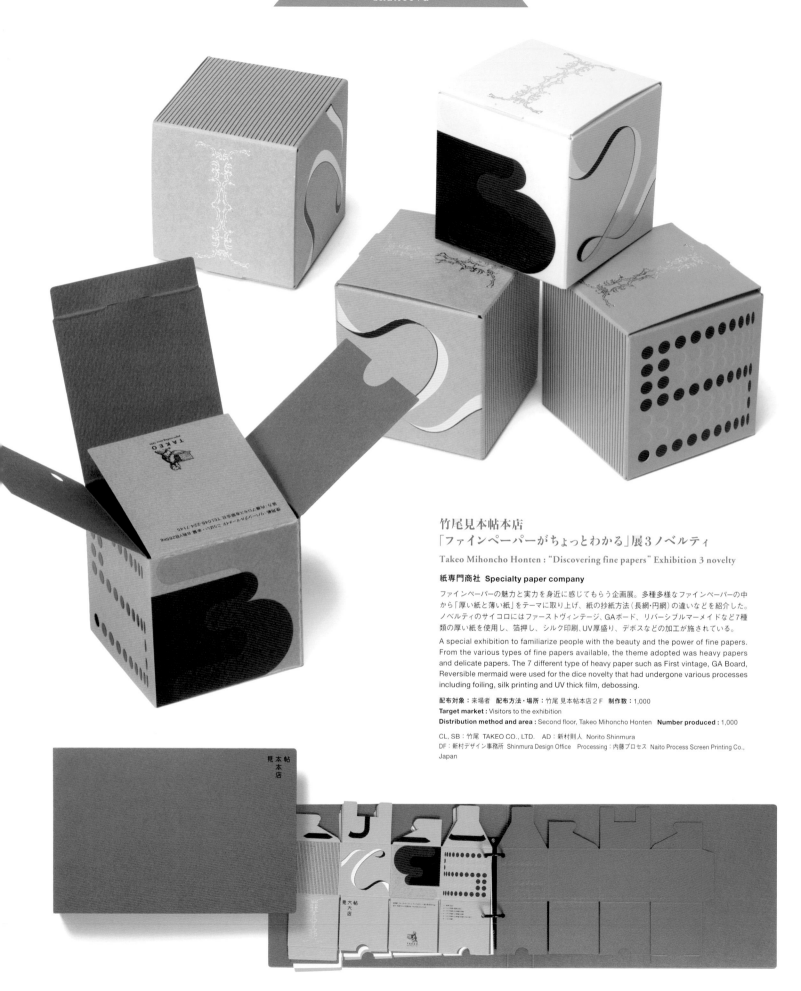

竹尾見本帖本店
「ファインペーパーがちょっとわかる」展3ノベルティ

Takeo Mihoncho Honten : "Discovering fine papers" Exhibition 3 novelty

紙専門商社 Specialty paper company

ファインペーパーの魅力と実力を身近に感じてもらう企画展。多種多様なファインペーパーの中から「厚い紙と薄い紙」をテーマに取り上げ、紙の抄紙方法（長網・円網）の違いなどを紹介した。ノベルティのサイコロにはファーストヴィンテージ、GAボード、リバーシブルマーメイドなど7種類の厚い紙を使用し、箔押し、シルク印刷、UV厚盛り、デボスなどの加工が施されている。

A special exhibition to familiarize people with the beauty and the power of fine papers. From the various types of fine papers available, the theme adopted was heavy papers and delicate papers. The 7 different type of heavy paper such as First vintage, GA Board, Reversible mermaid were used for the dice novelty that had undergone various processes including foiling, silk printing and UV thick film, debossing.

配布対象：来場者　配布方法・場所：竹尾 見本帖本店2F　制作数：1,000
Target market : Visitors to the exhibition
Distribution method and area : Second floor, Takeo Mihoncho Honten　**Number produced :** 1,000

CL, SB：竹尾 TAKEO CO., LTD.　AD：新村則人 Norito Shinmura
DF：新村デザイン事務所 Shinmura Design Office　Processing：内藤プロセス Naito Process Screen Printing Co., Japan

「竹尾ペーパーショウ 2008」プレスキット & ノベルティ

Takeo Paper Show 2008 : Press kit and novelty

紙専門商社 Specialty paper company

ファインペーパーを素材にそれぞれの用紙がもつ個性や機能を生かしたデザインをオリジナル文房具セットで表現・展示した「竹尾ペーパーショウ 2008」。プレスキットとして送られた箱の中には、ポスター（使用紙：バンクペーパー）と案内状（使用紙：ビオトープ コットンホワイト）が同封されている。来場者は、様々なファインペーパーを使用してデザインされた印刷見本を持ち帰ることができる。

The Takeo Paper Show 2008 with exhibits of actual products made from fine papers, with designs that exploit the characteristics and function of each of its papers. The box sent as the press kit contains a poster and an invitation to the exhibition. Visitors to the exhibition can take printed samples designed with various fine papers.

配布対象：プレス関係者・来場者　配布方法・場所：郵送・会場配布　制作数：300（プレスキット）
Target market : Media-related people and visitors　**Distribution method and area :** Distributed by mail and at exhibition venue　**Number produced :** 300 (press kit)

CL, SB：竹尾 TAKEO CO., LTD.　AD：SCHOOL OF DESIGN　Japan

アイルクリエイティブ「カップメール」

ayr creative "Cup mail"

デザイン Design

伝言メモとして製作された「カップメール」。内側にメッセージを書いて、カップにして組み立てて机に置くと、楽しく、遊び感覚で伝言を残すことができる。レモンティーの入ったカップや、ロックアイスの入ったコップなど絵柄もユニークなので、伝言を見る楽しみがふくらんで、コミュニケーションが楽しいものに変わる。

The cup email message was produced as a message card to be used by staff within the office. The message is written on the inside, the cup is then assembled and placed on someone's desk - a fun and playful way to leave someone a message. The cups come in a variety of unique patterns including tea with lemon or filled with ice cubes for an "on the rocks", and have become a useful tool for communication in the office.

CL, SB：アイルクリエイティブ ayr creative　AD, D：安田由美子 Yumiko Yasuda
D：岡崎智弘 Tomohiro Okazaki　P：西 将隆 Masataka Nishi　CW：武藤雄一 Yuichi Muto
Printing：大洋印刷 TAIYO PRINTING Co., Ltd.　Japan

スリーミン・グラフィック・アソシエイツ
シーズングリーティング
3 MIN. GRAPHIC ASSOCIATES : Seasons Greetings

グラフィックデザイン Graphic Design

東京のデザインユニット、スリーミン・グラフィック・アソシエイツがクライアントに感謝の気持ちを込めて贈るささやかなクリスマスプレゼント。真空パックされた銀色のパッケージには、季節のあいさつとグッズの使い方が英字で記され、中にはオリジナル鉛筆（2006年度版）や入浴剤（2007年度版）が入っている。アイテムを真空パックすることで、いつもとは違う見え方となり、開封する喜びも味わうことができる。

A small Christmas gift sent to client as an expression of its thanks. Season's greetings and instructions for using the goods are inscribed in English on the silver vacuum-packed package, and inside are bath products (2007 version) and an original pencil (2006 version). The contents were vacuum-packed to give the package an interesting look.

配布対象：クライアント　配布方法・場所：メール便　制作数：700個
狙い・効果：一年間のお礼を込めたクリスマスプレゼント
Target market : Clients **Distribution method and area :** Mail
Number produced : 700 **Aim and effect :** A Christmas present expressing thanks for the past year

CL, AD, SB：スリーミン・グラフィック・アソシエイツ
3MIN. GRAPHIC ASSOCIATES　Japan

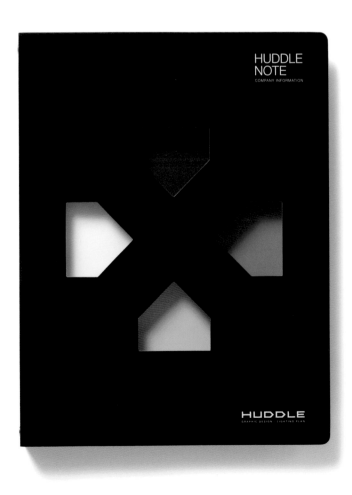

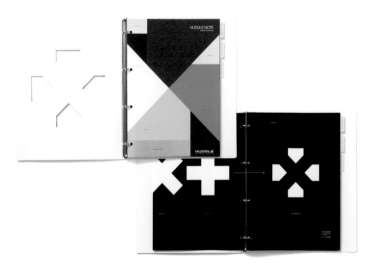

HUDDLE 事務所CIリニューアルに伴う営業ツール
Business tools for HUDDLE design office CI renewal

サイングラフィック・ライティングプランニング Sign graphics and lighting planning

サイングラフィック、ライティングプランなどを手がけるHUDDLEの会社案内。事務所CIリニューアルに伴い、事業拡大用の営業ツールとして製作された。造本は、後から自社のポートフォリオが追加できるように工夫したバインダー仕様とした。

Company profile for Huddle was produced as a business tool to be used in the expansion of HUDDLE's business, together with renewal of its corporate identity. The profile was placed in a binder so the company's portfolio could be added to at a later stage.

配布対象：顧客　配布方法・場所：営業先　制作数：300個
Target market : Clients **Distribution method and area :** Business partners **Number produced :** 300

CL：ハドル HUDDLE　CD, CW：水間 隆 Takashi Mizuma　AD, D：古川智基 Tomoki Furukawa
DF, SB：サファリ SAFARI inc.　Japan

KesselsKramer 事務所販促ノベルティ
Office novelty for KesselsKramer

広告制作 Communication agency

自社の「電話保留メッセージ」を集めたCDという奇想天外なPRツール。「電話を保留にされて待つ時間は、一生のうち2ヶ月にも相当する。当社に電話した人は保留中も楽しんでほしい」とユニークな保留音を使うケッセルズクレイマー。これは保留音10例を収録したCD。「楽しい待ち時間を擬似体験してほしい。このCDなら保留音の後、誰かと話す煩わしさもなし！」

On Hold at KesselsKramer re-lives those memorable moments when you were left dangling. The average person spend about 2 months of his or her life on hold. Ten call messages are included in the CD, without irritating need to talk with someone after.

配布対象：クライアント　制作数：500個
Target market : Clients　**Number produced :** 500

CL, DF, SB：KesselsKramer　CD, AD：Ewoudt Boonstra
D, I：Anthony Burrill　CW：Tyler Whisnand
Print producer：Noor van Geloven　RTV producer：Poeiwzah
Cheung　Sound：Park Studio / FC Walvisch　The Netherlands

「グッドデザイン・プレゼンテーション 2007」公式グッズ
"Good Design Presentation 2007" : Official goods

デザインフェア Design fair

グッドデザイン賞の一次審査を通過した作品を展示するデザインフェア「グッドデザイン・プレゼンテーション2007」の公式グッズ。この年は、オリジナルTシャツとオリジナルウォーター、ステッカーが製作された。ウォーターは会場にて2万本を配布、Tシャツは専門のサイトにて数量限定で販売された。

Official goods of the Good Design Presentation 2007 design fair, exhibiting the work that passed the first round of the Good Design Award competition. This year, an original T-shirt, original bottled water and stickers were produced. Twenty thousand bottles of the water were distributed at the event venue and a limited number of the T-shirts were sold on the website dedicated to the event.

配布対象：来場者　配布方法・場所：イベント会場
Target market : Visitors to the exhibition
Distribution method and area : Event venue
CL：日本産業デザイン振興会 Japan Industrial Design Promotion Organization
AD, D：青木克憲 Katsunori Aoki　I：寄藤文平 Bunpei Yorifuji
DF, SB：バタフライ・ストローク butterfly・stroke inc.　Japan

144

クリアファイル Clear file

たき工房 C.I　TAKI CORPORATION : Corporate identity

広告制作　Advertising production

TAKIの「T」をモチーフにしたシンボルマークは、人のシルエットを連想させるようデザイン。「スタッフ一人ひとりがキーパーソン（鍵）となり、未来への扉を開く」という意志が込められている。シンボルカラーには、いつまでも色あせずに輝き続ける「黄色」を採用。黄色がもつ明るくポジティブなイメージが、未来へと歩み続けるたき工房の先進性を表現している。

The TAKI CORPORATION symbol that uses the T of TAKI as a motif is designed to resemble a human silhouette, incorporating the idea that every staff member is a key person and opens the door to the future. Yellow has been used for the symbol, a color that forever remains bright. The aim was to overlay the positive and cheerful image of the color yellow onto TAKI CORPORATION's attitude towards its work.

配布対象：クライアント・関係者　**Target market :** Clients and related persons

CL, SB：たき工房 TAKI CORPORATION　AD, D：内田真弓 Mayumi Uchida　Printing：大洋印刷 TAIYO PRINTING CO., LTD.　Other：リ・デザイン・プロジェクト Re Design Project　Japan

「relax」定期購読者 ノベルティ
"relax"：Regular subscribers' novelty

出版　Publishing

雑誌「relax」（現在、休刊中）の定期購読者にプレゼントされたペンケース。TGB design.の石浦氏によるグラフィカルなデザインとなっている。

A pen case presented to regular subscribers of the magazine "relax" (not currently in publication). The graphic design is by Ishiura of TGB design.

配布対象：定期購読者　**Target market :** Regular subscribers

CL：マガジンハウス Magazine House Ltd.
AD, D：石浦 克 Masaru Ishiura　DF, SB：TGB design.　Japan

145

「retired weapons」イベントグッズ

"retired weapons" : Event goods

デザインプロジェクト Design project

アートディレクター・徳田祐司とプロデューサー・石川淳哉が2005年に始めたピースアートプロジェクト。21世紀の新しいピースマークとして、ピストルや戦車の銃口が曲がり、そこから花を咲かせた兵器のグラフィックを、誰もが直感で感じることができるようなシンプルなデザインにおとしこんでいる。

A peace art project launched by art director, Yuji Tokuda and producer, Junya Ishikawa in 2005. As a new peace mark for the 21st century, they have produced a simple, intuitive graphic design featuring a pistol and a tank with their muzzles turned upwards and sprouting flowers.

配布対象：世界中の人々 配布方法・場所：ショップ・ウェブ・展覧会・郵送等
狙い・効果：ピースへの願いを育み、対話のきっかけを作る
Target market : People throughout the world
Distribution method and area : Stores, web, exhibitions, mail etc.
Aim and effect : Nurture a desire for peace and create opportunities for discussion

CL：retired weapons   AD：徳田祐司 Yuji Tokuda（canaria inc.）
Producer：石川淳哉 Junya Ishikawa（junya ishikawa.com）
Agency, SB：canaria inc.   Japan

146

「see you again」イベントグッズ "see you again": Event goods

デザインプロジェクト Design project

「ゴミ問題をデザインでどう解決できるか」というテーマで20人のアーティストが参加したエキシビション「Treasured Trash Project」への出品作品。作品のタイトル「see you again」は、捨てるという行為が最後の別れではなく、「いつかどこかで会おう」という気持ちとイマジネーションにより人とゴミとの間に新たな関係が生まれると信じている、ということを伝えている。

A work exhibited in the exhibition "Treasured Trash Project" in which 20 artists participated, with the theme "how to solve the problem of rubbish through design." The title of the work, See You Again, conveys the idea that the act of throwing something away does not mean that you never see it again, and that the idea of "We'll meet again, somewhere, sometime" creates a new relationship between humans and rubbish.

配布対象：来場者　配布方法・場所：イベント会場
Target market : Visitors to the exhibition　**Distribution method and area :** Event venue

CL : Treasured Trash Project　AD : 徳田祐司 Yuji Tokuda (canaria inc.)　Agency, SB : canaria inc.　Japan

「金ケシ2007」コピーライター養成講座
受講記念ノベルティ
"Golden eraser 2007": Copywriting training course souvenir novelty

出版 Publishing

2004年より毎年、都築 徹クラスで配布されている金のカバー付き消しゴム。ダメなコピーを書いたワースト10人の生徒に渡されるため、もらった生徒が泣き出すなど、あまり良い印象を持たれていなかった。そこで2007年版では、たくさんの言葉が散りばめられたカバー付き本型ケースにセットできる仕様にし、不名誉なグッズでありながら講師の愛情が感じられるものに改良されている。

An eraser with a gold cover awarded each year since 2004 to students of Toru Tsuzuki's class. The eraser has somewhat of a bad name as it is presented to the ten students who produced the worst copy during the course. The 2007 version, therefore, was designed to be set into a book-shaped case with a cover with many encouraging messages inscribed, the expression of their teacher's regards makes the students feel better.

配布対象：講座でダメなコピーを書いた生徒　配布方法・場所：講座の授業内　制作数：10個
狙い・効果：不名誉なグッズでありながら、毎年デザインを変えることで受講生が欲しいグッズとなることを目指した。
Target market : To students who produced the worst copy during the course **Distribution method and area :** During classes
Number produced : 10 **Aim and effect :** By changing the design each year, to make the eraser, paradoxically, an object of desire for the students.

CL：宣伝会議コピーライター養成講座名古屋教室 都築徹クラス
　　Sendenkaigi Copywriter School Nagoya, Tsuzuki Toru Class
AD, D：平井秀和 Hidekazu Hirai　CW：都築 徹 Toru Tsuzuki
DF, SB：ピースグラフィックス Peace Graphics
Printing：伊藤美藝社 Ito Bigei　Japan

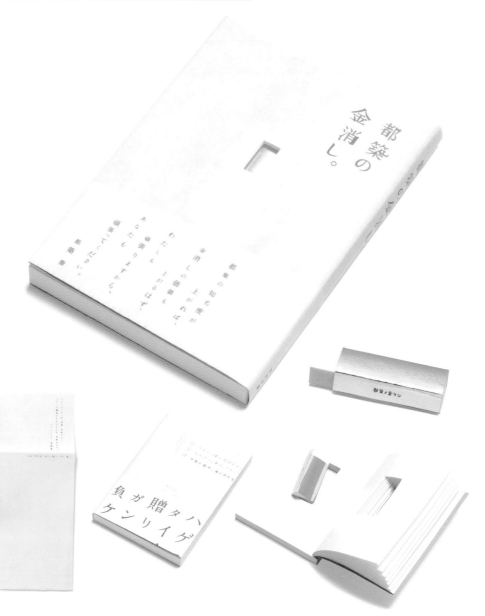

「金ケシ2008」コピーライター養成講座
受講記念ノベルティ
"Golden eraser 2008": Copywriting training course souvenir novelty

出版 Publishing

自動車プラグや化粧品の箱を連想させるレトロテイストな箱入り。高級感が感じられるよう、全て箔押し加工を施している。中には「使い方説明書」と称する、コピーを書く際の注意点が表記された紙が入っている。毎年デザインが一新される「金ケシ」は、当初のネガティブなイメージから一転、いまや受講生の誰もが欲しがるレア・アイテムとなっている。

Boxes in a retro style that are reminiscent of car plug or cosmetics boxes. Gold leaf has been applied to all the boxes for a luxury look. Inside is an instruction manual containing advice for writing your own copy. The Golden Eraser that is redesigned each year has moved away from its initial sombre image to become a much sought after item by all the students in the course.

配布対象：講座でダメなコピーを書いた生徒　配布方法・場所：講座の授業内　制作数：10個
Target market : Students who produced poor copy during the course
Distribution method and area : During classes **Number produced :** 10

CL：宣伝会議コピーライター養成講座名古屋教室 都築徹クラス
　　Sendenkaigi Copywriter School Nagoya, Tsuzuki Toru Class
AD, D：平井秀和 Hidekazu Hirai　CW：都築 徹 Toru Tsuzuki
DF, SB：ピースグラフィックス Peace Graphics
Printing：伊藤美藝社 Ito Bigei　Japan

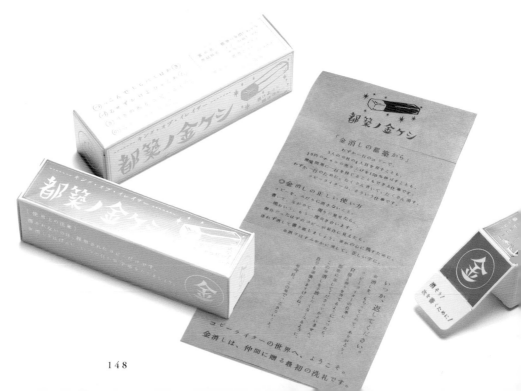

「オモシロ・エコアイデア 100 連発」 ノベルティブック

A novelty book of "100 Intersting Eco Ideas

グラフィックデザイン Graphic design

エコライフスタイルの実践につながる気づきときっかけづくりを目的としたイベント「Soul Switch in Marunouchi」の一環として、水野学率いるデザイン事務所「good design company」のスタッフが考案したエコにつながる100のアイデアを展示した「オモシロ・エコアイデア100連発」展の作品を一冊にまとめたノベルティブック。会場にて冊数限定で配布された。

A novelty book that is a compilation of work from the "100 Interesting Eco Ideas" exhibition that featured 100 ideas relating to ecology thought up by staff members of the design firm "good design company" which is headed by Manabu Mizuno, as part of the event "Soul Switch in Marunouchi," the aim of which was to create awareness of and an opportunity for practicing an eco-lifestyle. A limited number of the books were distributed at the event venue.

配布対象：イベント来場者 **Target market :** Visitors to the event
AD：水野 学 Manabu Mizuno
D, DF, SB：グッドデザインカンパニー good design company Japan

JAGDA
「グラフィックデザイナーの富嶽三十六景」ノベルティ

JAGDA : "Graphic designer's 36 Views of Mount Fuji" novelty

デザイン団体 Design association

富士山をテーマとしたアートポスター展のノベルティとしてTシャツやメモパッド、リーフレットなどを作成。日本の伝統的なデザートであるかき氷で富士山を表現し、キービジュアルとして各ツールにおとしこんだ。

T-shirts, memo pads and leaflets among other things were produced as novelties for an art poster exhibition featuring the theme of Mount Fuji. Mount Fuji was expressed with the traditional Japanese dessert of chipped ice, which was then incorporated into each of the tools as a key visual.

配布対象：展覧会来場者 配布方法・場所：展覧会会場 狙い・効果：プロモーションと来場促進
制作コスト：約15万円
Target market : Visitors to the exhibition **Distribution method and area :** Exhibition venue
Aim and effect : Promotion and increasing traffic **Production cost :** Approx. ¥150,000

CL：日本グラフィックデザイナー協会 Japan Graphic Designers Association Inc.
CD：明富士治郎 Jiro Akefuji AD, D：池澤 樹 Tatsuki Ikezawa P：井上佐由紀 Sayuki Inoue
Retouch：望月洋輔 Yosuke Mochizuki CW：中里智史 Satoshi Nakazato
Agency, SB：東急エージェンシー Tokyu Agency Inc. Printing：ラスター lasterInc. Japan

トーキョウ・グレート・ヴィジュアル
2008年 年賀状「2007年 作品集」

Tokyo Great Visual 2008 New Year's Card "2007 Anthology"

ブランディング・コミュニケーションデザイン
Branding and communication design

毎年、オリジナルのツールと作品集が収められたDVDをセットにして、クライアントや関係者に送っているトーキョウ・グレート・ヴィジュアル。「KEEP BLUE」というコンセプトから、2008年は「藍」、「群青色」、「シアン・ブルー」などあらゆるブルーを使用した美しいかたを制作。伝統的なアイテムを作り、プレゼントすることで、手作りの大切さを改めて認識できるよう心がけている。

Tokyo Great Visual a set of DVDs containing original tools and an anthology sent out to clients and related persons every year. From the concept called "Keep Blue," in 2008 an exquisite set of playing cards was produced in a range of blues including indigo, navy and cyan. A traditional item that again reminds us of the value of the hand-made.

配布対象：クライアント・関係者　配布方法・場所：郵送　制作数：1,000部
狙い・効果：水があり、大気があり、生物が宿る 青い星、地球。青は、豊かな生命力を象徴する色なのかも知れない。紺碧の海、藍色に染まる空、鮮やかな青瑠璃の花。人の暮らしのもっとも身近にあり、その地の風土をかたちづくる。私たちは、大いなるインスピレーションを与えてくれるその普遍的な色を生かしながら、一歩先の未来設計をめざしている。
Target market : Clients, related persons　Distribution method and area : Mail
Number produced : 1,000　Aim and effect : The blue planet, Earth, where there is water, where there is air, where living creatures dwell. Perhaps the color blue symbolizes life force. Azure sea, indigo-stained skies, flowers the color of lapis lazuli: blue is the most familiar color in people's lives, the color that shapes a place's climate. Drawing on this universal color that provides great inspiration, we strive for future design...one step ahead.

CL, AD, D, I, CW, SB：トーキョウ・グレート・ヴィジュアル　TOKYO GREAT VISUAL
CD：内藤久幹 Hisamoto Naitou　Japan

SPECIAL CONTENTS　特集

ノベルティの基礎知識

Basic tips for producing novelty goods

アイテム決定と、予算や時間
Deciding what to make, how much to spend and how long to take

作りたいアイテムがはっきりしている場合は、具体的な予算と個数、また納期を調べて調整します。最低価格と個数を複数の業者から見積り、予算に合わない場合は、色数を減らしたり、印刷の場合は付け合わせ(面付け)を工夫することで価格を抑えることもできます。具体的には業者に相談するのがいいでしょう。アイテムが決まらない場合は、予算や個数から考えることも可能です。その場合は、右の表を参考にしてください。いずれの場合も納期を考慮することを忘れてはいけません。アイテムによって制作期間は異なりますが、印刷物ならば1～2週間、それ以外は2～4週間はみておきましょう。また中国などの海外生産は、試作確認なども必要なため、1カ月以上を要することもあります。

When you are clear about what you want to make, then prepare your budget and decide on the number of units and delivery deadline. Get estimates from a range of suppliers to find the lowest price and number of units, and where the estimates don't come in under budget, find ways of adjusting costs, for example by reducing the number of colors or in the case of printed materials, by repagination. It is advisable to discuss the details with the supplier. If you haven't decided what you want to make, you can consider your options according to your budget and number of units. If this is the case, use the table above. In either case, do not forgot to consider the deadline for delivery. Production times vary according to what is being produced, but set aside around 1 - 2 weeks for printed materials and around 2 - 4 weeks for others things. If you are having your items manufactured overseas, in China for example, you will be required to sign off a prototype among other things, all of which may take a month or longer.

配布する目的や対象を明確に
Be clear about why you are distributing novelty goods and to whom you are distributing them

ノベルティグッズを作る際、もっとも大切なことは、配布する目的と対象者(ターゲット)を明確にすることです。新商品をPRするにしても、「まず、商品名を知ってもらいたい」のか、「従来のものより製品が向上したことを知ってほしいのか」など、目的はさまざまです。また、ターゲットを意識することで、作るアイテムもおのずと年齢や性別に即したものになるはずです。これらを見誤ると、"誰も欲しがらない、不要なもの"を生み出してしまいます。環境にも配慮し、"いらないものは作らない"という意識も持っておきましょう。

If The most important thing when producing novelty goods is to be clear about your purpose for distributing them and the people you are targeting. Even where they are to serve as publicity for a new product, novelty goods have various purposes, for example getting the product's name out there among consumers or telling consumers that your product is better than other products of the same kind. Being aware of who you are targeting means that novelty goods can be tailored according to age group and sex. Otherwise you run the risk of producing something useless that nobody wants. For the sake of the environment, let's be aware of the fact that making something that nobody wants is not a good idea.

配布方法を考えて梱包を
Package your novelty goods according to distribution method

飴やチョコなどを配る場合、1粒ずつ配るのか5粒ひとまとめにして配るのかなどによって、手間や配布方法が異なります。どのようなシーンで配布するのかを考慮し、袋詰めや梱包なども考えておきましょう。こうしたアイデアは、一般的に専門業者ほど得意といえます。見積もりを比較する際、金額だけで比べず、こうした後加工オプションも含めて検討することが重要です。

If you are distributing candy or chocolate, the time involved in producing the novelty goods and the distribution method will vary according to whether, for example, you are distributing one piece of candy or chocolate or five pieces. Consider the setting for distribution of your novelty goods before deciding on the kind of packaging, be that bagged or wrapped in some other way. Coming up with ideas for packaging is generally the forte of specialist suppliers. It is important to consider such options for post-production, and not just to think in terms of price when comparing estimates.

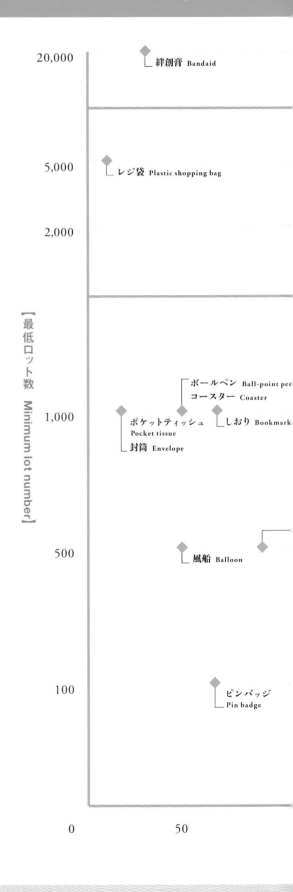

アイテム別　最低ロット数・単価
Minimum lot number / unit price by item

【最低ロット数　Minimum lot number】

- 20,000　絆創膏 Bandaid
- 5,000　レジ袋 Plastic shopping bag
- 2,000
- ボールペン Ball-point pen
- コースター Coaster
- 1,000　ポケットティッシュ Pocket tissue　しおり Bookmark　封筒 Envelope
- 500　風船 Balloon
- 100　ピンバッジ Pin badge
- 0
- 50

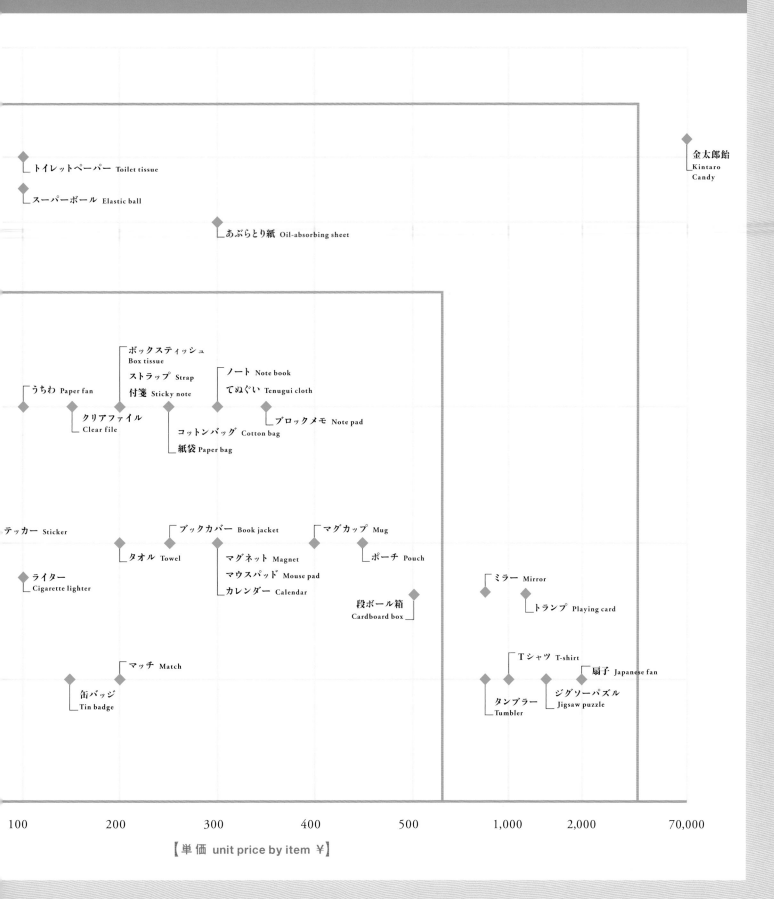

トイレットペーパー Toilet tissue
スーパーボール Elastic ball
あぶらとり紙 Oil-absorbing sheet
金太郎飴 Kintaro Candy

ボックスティッシュ Box tissue
ストラップ Strap
付箋 Sticky note
ノート Note book
てぬぐい Tenugui cloth
ブロックメモ Note pad
うちわ Paper fan
クリアファイル Clear file
コットンバッグ Cotton bag
紙袋 Paper bag

テッカー Sticker
ブックカバー Book jacket
マグカップ Mug
タオル Towel
マグネット Magnet
マウスパッド Mouse pad
カレンダー Calendar
ポーチ Pouch
ライター Cigarette lighter
段ボール箱 Cardboard box
ミラー Mirror
トランプ Playing card
マッチ Match
缶バッジ Tin badge
Tシャツ T-shirt
扇子 Japanese fan
タンブラー Tumbler
ジグソーパズル Jigsaw puzzle

| 100 | 200 | 300 | 400 | 500 | 1,000 | 2,000 | 70,000 |

【 単価 unit price by item ￥】

【グッズ制作会社一覧】

各制作会社では、下記に記載のあるアイテム以外にも取り扱っている場合があります。
詳細は、各制作会社のホームページ、または窓口にお問い合わせください。
Production companies deal in items other than the ones mentioned below. For further details, visit the supplier's website or contact them.

会社名	アイテム名	最低ロット数	単価
アドアチーブ(株) / adACHIEVE co.,ltd.	Tシャツ	1枚〜	298円〜
	不織布バッグ	100枚〜	約113円（不織布バッグ・手さげ4,800枚の場合）
	シール・ステッカー	500枚〜	約18円（50mm×50mm・フルカラー 3,000枚の場合）
	クリアファイル	500部〜	約36円（箔押し印刷3,000部の場合）
(株)アトミ / ATOMI CO., Ltd.	カタログ	100部〜	
	ポスター	100部〜	
	DM	100部〜	
	インビテーション	100部〜	
	カレンダー	100部〜	
(株)イメージ・マジック / IMAGEMAGIC Inc.	アルミカードケース	1個	〜 1,543円
	B6リングノート	1個	〜 724円
	アルミスクエアミラー	1個	〜 1,338円
	缶バッジ (31mm)	1個	〜 215円
	ボールペン (10本セット)	1個	〜 1,470円
(株)エイチ・エヌ・アンド・アソシエイツ / HN & Associates CO., LTD.	フィギュア類	1,000個〜	
	プレート類	1,000個〜	
	ストラップ・ネックストラップ	1,000個〜	
	ぬいぐるみ	1,000個〜	
(株)小樽キャスト製作所 / Otaru Cast	オリジナル直火式焼印（食品用深彫 L 型直火式）	1個	3,150円〜
	オリジナル電気ゴテ式焼印	1個	4,620円〜（電気ゴテ代含む）
(株)金太郎飴本店 / Kintarou-ame Honten	オリジナル飴（面切タイプ）	1種類、約1,500粒（バラ納品不可）	35,000円
	オリジナル飴（ピロータイプ）	1種類、約6,000粒（バラ納品可）	70,000円
久世産業(株) / Kuze Industry Co., Ltd.	バッグ		
	ステッカー		
(株)グラビティ / Glavity Co., Inc.	ステッカー (サイズA25)	100枚	5.25円
	Tシャツ	10枚 / 100枚	1,000円〜 / 100 〜 300円
	転写式シール (ハガキサイズ)	100枚	9,870円（2009年3月まで限定）
(有)クリエイト / CREATE	オリジナル紙袋	1,000枚〜	98円〜
(株)コーエイトレード / Koei Trade Co., Ltd.			
三和タオル製織(株) / Sanwa Towel	シャーリングマフラータオル（顔料1色プリント）	100枚	483円〜
	シャーリングフェイスタオル（顔料1色プリント）	100枚	423円〜
	日本てぬぐい（顔料1色プリント）	100枚	343円〜
	シャーリングスポーツタオル（顔料1色プリント）	100枚	568円〜
	シャーリングミニタオル（顔料1色プリント）	100枚	278円〜
	※各商品は、1枚からでも注文可能		
(株)シップス / CIPS co., Ltd.	MOSMOS (パッケージDM)	500部〜	約200円〜
大日紙業(株) / Dainichi	ピクチャーブロックメモ	100個	見積もり相談対応
	カットメモ	500個	見積もり相談対応
	ダイカットメモ（型抜きメモ）	1,000個	見積もり相談対応
	温度計つきPOP−UPメモ	1,000個	見積もり相談対応
	たまーるぺんたてティッシュ（筒型ティッシュ兼ぺんたて）	1,000個	見積もり相談対応
(株)竹尾 / TAKEO CO., LTD.	竹尾デザイン封筒	原紙1枚からの取数。洋2封筒の場合8部〜	加工代＋紙代（見積もり相談対応）
	NOTE BOOK (Dressco型)	1,000個	約800円〜（要見積もり）
	BOOKMARKBAND（ゴムバンドつきシオリ）	500部	約300円〜（要見積もり）
ツユキ紙工(株) / Tsuyuki	オリジナルトイレットペーパー		
(株)東洋レーベル / Toyo Label	蒔絵シール (3×3センチ)	1,000枚〜	
(株)トランス / TRANS			
(株)日東社 / Nittosha Co.,Ltd.	マッチ	100個〜	188円〜
	ポケットティッシュ	1,000個〜	見積もり相談対応
	粘着メモ	200個〜	見積もり相談対応
	フルカラーのぼり	1枚〜	見積もり相談対応
ハグルマ封筒(株) / HAGURUMA ENVELOPE Co., LTD			
(有)バッファロー・レコード / Buffalo Records	greensticks 5本入り	2,000個〜	
	greensticks 10本入り	1,000個〜	

住所	TEL & FAX	E-mail & URL	担当部署・担当者名	備考
大阪市中央区南久宝寺町3-2-7 第一住建南久宝寺町ビル7F	06-6281-5103 06-6281-5104	info@a-ac.jp http://www.a-ac.jp	グラフィックデザイン部 遠山展生	
東京都小平市小川東町5-13-22	042-345-1155 042-343-3517	info@atomi.co.jp http://www.atomi.co.jp	営業部	
東京都新宿区市谷左内町29-3	03-5228-1062 03-5228-1060	tachikawa@imagemagic.co.jp http://create.upsold.com	upsold事業部 太刀川 淳	
静岡県静岡市駿河区中原584-1	054-283-1333 054-283-1132	info_siz@hna.co.jp http://www.hna.co.jp		
北海道小樽市梅ヶ枝町40番4号	0134-32-0550 0134-32-0550	info@otaru-cast.com http://www.otaru-cast.com	梶原三央	
東京都台東区根岸5-16-12	03-3872-7706 03-3872-7785	info@kintarou.co.jp http://www.kintarou.co.jp	渡辺朋子	5粒より袋詰め可能。
東京都渋谷区神宮前1-21-3 アローマンション103号 203号	03-3470-0404 03-3402-1335	kuze@kuzenet.co.jp http://www.kuzenet.co.jp		完全オーダーメイド制。
東京都杉並区天沼2-4-1 井上ビル3号館3F	03-5347-2963 03-5347-2471	flyer@glavity.com http://www.glavity.com	堀越	
大阪市中央区森ノ宮中央1丁目14-2 鵲森ノ宮ビル4F	06-4790-8771 06-4790-8772	info@paper-bag.jp http://www.paper-bag.jp	谷元	
大阪市中央区大手前1-7-31 OMMビル12F	06-6910-5500 06-6910-5501	info@hansokuhin.com http://www.hansokuhin.com		
京都府福知山市三和町字菟原下166	0773-58-2218 0773-58-2249	sanwatowel@original-towel.jp http://www.original-towel.jp	オリジナルタオルを 作りま専科	単価は、顔料プリントし、100枚ポリ袋入りにした場合の参考価格。各商品は、1枚からでも注文可能。
大阪市北区本庄西2-1-31	06-6377-1350 06-6377-1363	info@mosmos.co.jp http://www.mosmos.co.jp	MOSMOS事業部 黒木	
静岡県静岡市葵区流通センター12-1	054-263-2435 054-263-2409	matsunaga@skp-net.com http://www.dainichi-p.co.jp	第二販売事業部 商品企画・IT推進課 松永桂一	
東京都千代田区神田錦町3-12-6	見本帖本店： 03-3292-3669 / 03-3292-3668 TAKEO PAPER PRODUCTS Dressco： 03-3292-3280 / 03-3292-3667	見本帖本店：mihon@takeo.co.jp TAKEO PAPER PRODUCTS Dressco： info@dressco.jp http://www.takeo.co.jp		
静岡県富士市今泉383-1	0545-51-0866 0545-55-0866	tsuyuki@tsuyuki.co.jp http://www.tsuyuki.co.jp	オリジナル担当 露木祐一郎	オーダーメイドのトイレットペーパーを1個から作れる。
京都市右京区西京極畑田町8	075-314-2117 075-313-4652	info@toyolabel.co.jp http://www.toyolabel.co.jp		
東京都渋谷区渋谷3-28-13 渋谷新南口ビル9F	03-5468-9411 03-5468-9894	info@transcom.co.jp http://www.trans.co.jp		
兵庫県姫路市東山524	079-246-1561 079-246-1159	100ko@nitto-sha.co.jp http://www.nitto-sha.co.jp	管理本部 神村昌樹	
大阪市中央区南船場2-12-10-4F	0120-890-982 0120-890-883	info@haguruma.co.jp http://www.haguruma.co.jp/index.html	井谷	ロット数、値段は同社HPのオンラインショップを参照。
神奈川県鎌倉市材木座1-10-37 グレースガーデン101	0467-23-3778 0467-61-1397	seeds@greensticks.jp http://www.greensticks.jp	グリーンスティック事業部	単価など、詳細は問い合わせが必要。

▶グッズ制作会社一覧

会社名	アイテム名	最低ロット数	単価
BA - PrintActive	Tシャツ	1枚〜	版代（シルクスクリーン）：5,000円〜10,000円　量産単価：1,000円〜
	エコバッグ	1袋〜	600円〜
平林印刷(株)＜販促花子＞ / Hirabayashi print Co.,ltd.	うちわ	100個〜	295円〜
	卓上カレンダー	100個〜	450円〜
	おまメッセージ（豆の両面にメッセージの入った鉢植え）	100個〜	315円〜
	ビーチサンダル	3,000個〜	205円〜
	イヤホン	500個	750円〜
(株)デザインアンドディベロップメント ＜ピンズファクトリー＞ / Design and Development.Co.,LTD. ＜PINS FACTORY＞	ピンバッジ（ピンズパック100）	100個	57,750円
	社章（社章パック）	50個	73,500円
	ショートストラップ（ピンズパック100＋オプション）	100個	68,250円
	ファスナーマスコット（ピンズパック100＋オプション）	100個	68,250円
	ゴルフのクリップマーカー（クリップマーカーかんたんパック）	50個	81,000円
(有)プラネッツ＜ふろしきや＞ / Plant.Inc.＜Furoshikiya＞	風呂敷（プリント1色 レーヨン100%、45×45cm）	1枚	6,200円〜
	風呂敷（プリント1色 レーヨン100%、68×68cm）	1枚	6,600円〜
	風呂敷（染め1色 レーヨン100%、68×68cm）	100枚	1,900円〜
	風呂敷（染め1色 綿100%、90×90cm）	100枚	1,950円〜
	てぬぐい（染め1色 綿100%、34×90cm）	100枚	550円〜
ホリアキ(株) / HORIAKI Co.,Ltd.	ゴムバンド（折径80mm切幅3mm、2層・3層タイプ）	1,000本〜	約20円
	ゴムバンド（折径140mm切幅3mm、2層・3層タイプ）	1,000本〜	約35円
	サボン ドゥ フルール ローズアーチケース入り	30箱	450円（通常販売価格、定価は750円）
	サボン ドゥ フルール ローズアーチケース入り（パワーストンシリーズ）	30箱	600円（通常販売価格、定価は1,000円）
増成織ネーム(株) / Masunari Woven Label.Co.,Ltd.	モバイルクリーナー	300個	約160円〜（版代など固定費別途）
	ネックストラップ	100本	約600円〜
	エコバッグ	1,000枚	350円〜
	お守り	300個	200円〜（型代50,000円別途必要）
	ジャガードタオル	300〜400枚	120円〜
(株)マック / MAQ inc.	GARBAGE BAG ART WORK アートゴミ袋 (a)	30,000枚〜	22円〜
	GARBAGE BAG ART WORK MYゴミ持ち帰り袋（Love it!!君 マナーバッグ）	30,000枚〜	20円〜
	オリジナルアートゴミ袋 (b)	応相談	応相談
(株)マックスタイル / MAC STYLE	DECOチョコ（http://www.decocho.com/）	1セット（45個）	2,362円（消費税込み・送料別）
	プロフ-ハイチュウ（http://www.pro-chew.jp）	1箱（12個）	2,520円（消費税込み・送料別）
(株)マルオカ / Maruoka Co.,Ltd.	ペーパーコースター	5,000枚〜	5円〜
	ペーパーナプキン	10,000枚〜	0.60円〜
	ペーパーフレグランス	1枚×120パック	100円〜
	紙おしぼり	1,600本〜	3.5円〜
	Duni ペーパーナプキン	20枚〜	500円 / 1パック
(株)マルジュー / MARUJU Co., Ltd.	オリジナルプリントのファブリックグッズ	1点〜	
(株)マルモ印刷 / Marumo	ファイルDEメール 封筒タイプ （手で切り取ると、クリアファイルとして再使用できるPP製封筒）	500枚〜	見積もり相談対応
	ファイルDEメール バッグタイプタイプ （手で切り取ると、クリアファイルとして再使用できるPP製バッグ）	500枚〜	見積もり相談対応
森実商事(株) / Morizane shoji Co.,ltd.	オリジナルBoxティッシュ	100個〜	約400円〜
	ローション ブラック・レッドBoxティッシュ ROSE	4個〜	420円
	ローション ブラック・レッドポケットティッシュ（4個入り）	10パック〜	160円
	オリジナル ポケットティッシュ	1,000個	約30円〜
(株)ヤギセイ / YAGISEI Co., Ltd.	プリントてぬぐい（日本製、34×90cm）	500枚〜	約85円〜
	注染てぬぐい（日本製、34×90cm）	300枚〜	約250円〜
	シャーリングタオル ミニハンカチ（日本製、20×20cm）	1,000枚〜	約85円〜
	風呂敷（綿シャンタン、日本製、50×50cm）	1,000枚〜	約160円〜
	風呂敷（ポリエステルチリメン、中国製、50×50cm）	1,0000枚〜	約100円〜
(株)山元紙包装社 / Yamamoto Kamihousousha.co.,ltd.	手さげ袋	100枚〜	約200円
	不織布バッグ	100枚〜	約250円
	エコバッグ	100枚〜	約200円
	手さげポリ袋	1,000枚〜	約40円
	キャンバストートバッグ	100枚〜	約300円
リード工業(株) / Reed	メモ帳		
	カレンダー		
リンテック(株) / LINTEC CORPORATION	フィットメイトカレンダー（台座部に箔押し名入れ）	100部	600円
	フィットメイトD100タイプ（表紙に箔押し名入れ）	500部	210円
	フィットメイトD100タイプ（表紙・裏表紙にオフセット4色印刷）	500部	300円
	フィットメイトダイアリー（のりつき台紙に1色入れた挿入台紙つき）	1,000部	320円
	フィットメイトタッタ（用紙にオフセット1色印刷）	1,000部	280円

住所	TEL & FAX	E-mail & URL	担当部署・担当者名	備考
東京都渋谷区富ヶ谷2-8-1-1F	03-5738-3216 03-5738-3219	paku@ba-p-co.jp http://www.ba-p-co.jp/printactive	松林	
福井県福井市長本町220-1	0776-57-0875 0776-57-0045	info@hi-ad.jp http://www.hi-ad.jp	営業 皆川友美	
東京都港区三田4-15-35 7F	03-5441-7417 03-5441-7428	info@pins.co.jp http://www.pins.co.jp	企画営業グループ 依田一雄	いずれも、固定費込みのパック限定料金。
茨城県常陸大宮市北町91番地	0295-52-0041 0295-53-5578	ys3t-krt@asahi-net.or.jp http://www.rakuten.co.jp/furoshikiya	倉田稔之	
大阪府東大阪市長田中3-6-8	06-6747-5731 06-6745-9527	youshina@horiaki.co.jp http://www.horiaki.co.jp/package	企画開発部 用品孝浩	『サボンドゥフルール』は、せっけん素材で作られた花。アロマの香りが楽しめる。
東京都千代田区岩本町3-5-5 アーバンスクエアビル3F	03-3866-6780 03-3863-1940	info@masunari-net.co.jp http://www.masunari-net.co.jp	商品企画課 柴田眞義	小ロットでのオリジナル製品も作成可能。要望、用途、予算に応じて仕様の変更もできる。
東京都港区南青山4-17-3	03-5411-2646 03-5411-2640	yamasaka@maq.co.jp http://www.maq.co.jp http://www.maq.co.jp/gba	山阪佳彦	a,bはロゴ入れ可能。
東京都台東区浅草3-25-9	03-5824-1850	http://www.macstyle-net.jp	ユアスタイル事業部 田村	その他、文房具（ナルミヤインターナショナル・ライセンス商品など多数）の製造、販売を行っている。
東京都台東区浅草6-41-13	03-3876-3304 03-3876-3306	info@maruoka.com http://www.maruoka.com	営業部 須永 均	
愛知県名古屋市北区楠味鋺5-209	052-901-1966 052-901-7676	mail@maruju.net http://www.maruju.net		オリジナル商品はそれぞれ異なるため、単価はまちまち。
香川県三豊市豊中町笠田笠岡3915-5	0875-62-5856 0875-62-5861	info@marumo-print.co.jp http://www.marumo-print.co.jp	営業企画課 石井章弘	商標登録・意匠登録・PAT-P
東京都港区南青山2-4-16 ANNOビル2F	03-5474-9221 03-5474-9223	info@kamikau.com http://kamikau.com	営業部 土井秀陸	
大阪市中央区博労町1丁目4-10	06-6271-1531 06-6264-1532	marusenikko@yagisei.co.jp http://www.yagisei.co.jp	営業 林 秀樹	
大阪市都島区中野町2-9-3	06-6352-3031 06-6352-3034	info@yamagen-net.com http://www.yamagen-net.com	山元久良	
群馬県多野郡吉井町矢田1013	027-387-2807 03-3868-7739	reed.co@reed-s.com http://www.reed-s.com	松本	
東京都文京区後楽2-1-2 興和飯田橋ビル	03-3868-7733 03-3868-7739	http://www.fitmate.com	産業工材事業部門 コンシューマーグループ 宮本 浩	

CLIENT クライアント

SUBMITTOR 作品提供者

ノベルティ グラフィックス　Premium Novelties

Jacket Design

Art Director	えぐちりか（株式会社電通）	Rika Eguchi（DENTSU INC.）
Designer	阿部梨絵（株式会社電通）	Rie Abe（DENTSU INC.）
Photographer	佐藤博文（株式会社アキューブ）	Hirofumi Sato（acube Inc.）
Retoucher	吉川武志（株式会社アキューブ）	Takeshi Yoshikawa（acube Inc.）
Photo Producer	皆川哲哉（株式会社アマナ）	Tetsuya Minakawa（amana Inc.）

Art Director	柴 亜季子	Akiko Shiba
Designer	佐藤美穂	Miho Sato
Photographer	藤本邦治	Kuniharu Fujimoto
Coordinator & Writer	田端宏章	Hiroaki Tabata
	白倉三紀子	Mikiko Shirakuraa
	河村美智香	Michika Kawamur
	原田弥生	Yayoi Harada
Translator	三木アソシエイツ	Miki Associates
Editor	宮崎亜美	Ami Miyazaki
Publisher	三芳伸吾	Shingo Miyoshi

2009年2月17日　初版第1刷発行

PIE BOOKS

2-32-4, Minami-Otsuka, Toshima-ku, Tokyo 170-0005 Japan
Tel: +81-3-5395-4811 Fax: +81-3-5395-4812
e-mail: editor@piebooks.com
　　　　sales@piebooks.com
http://www.piebooks.com

発行所　ピエ・ブックス

〒170-0005　東京都豊島区南大塚2-32-4
編集 Tel: 03-5395-4820　Fax: 03-5395-4821
e-mail: editor@piebooks.com
営業 Tel: 03-5395-4811　Fax: 03-5395-4812
e-mail: sales@piebooks.com
http://www.piebooks.com

印刷・製本　株式会社サンニチ印刷

©2009 PIE BOOKS
ISBN978-4-89444-752-3 C3070
Printed in Japan